We are the Romani people
Ame sam e Rromane džene

We are the Romani people
Ame sam e Rromane džene

Ian Hancock

CENTRE DE RECHERCHES TSIGANES
UNIVERSITY OF HERTFORDSHIRE PRESS

The *Interface Collection* is co-ordinated and developed by the
Gypsy Research Centre at the Université René Descartes in Paris

The views expressed in this work are the authors and do not necessarily reflect those of the
publisher nor of the Gypsy Research Centre or its research groups
(historians, linguists, education specialists, etc.)

The Director of the *Interface Collection* is Jean-Pierre Liégeois

First published in Great Britain in 2002 by
University of Hertfordshire Press
Learning and Information Services
University of Hertfordshire
College Lane
Hatfield,
Hertfordshire AL10 9AB

Reprinted December 2003

ISBN 1 902806 19 0 paper back

British Library Cataloguing in Publication Data
A catalogue record for this book is available from the British Library

Design by Geoff Green, Cambridge CB4 5RA.
Cover design by John Robertshaw, Harpenden AL5 2JB
Printed in Great Britain by Antony Rowe Ltd, SN14 6LH

Frontispiece: The author standing next to a Reading waggon (photograph by Thomas Acton)

E serimatange murre dadeske

Contents

Foreword

Ken Lee

I am a *Romanichal*, born in a horse-drawn waggon in Ireland, raised and educated in England, now living in Australia.

As a child in England, I knew of 'foreign' Romanies, like us Romanichals but somehow different. I had heard my father and other Romanichals talk of 'foreign' Romanies they had travelled with in the 1930s. I had heard old Gordon Boswell talk of the 'foreign' Romanies he had traded horses with in Belgium before the First World War. I had heard Dora Yates, the gypsylorist, talk of 'foreign Gypsies', listening to her recollections of "the invasion of the German Gypsies" at Blackpool in 1906, and "the invasion of the Coppersmith Gypsies" at Liverpool in 1911. I had looked at some of her photographs of these exotic foreigners, bearded men in knee-boots, baggy pants, puff-sleeve shirts and big silver-buttoned coats, hammering copper bowls on stakes in the ground, women in ankle-length skirts and gold coin necklaces, boys dressed like their fathers, puffing on pipes and cigarettes. And of course I had read stories of the flamenco artists of Spain, the Romani orchestras of Hungary.

However, it wasn't until 1956 I first met 'foreign' Romanies, refugees from the Hungarian Revolution. A welfare agency had contacted a local gypsylorist, asking for translation assistance for the family of Hungarian Romanies. He in turn had contacted my father, and we all went to visit the family. They didn't look much like the people in the exotic photographs in Dora's office, and they were not what I imagined Hungarian Romanies to be like – no velvet waistcoats, no violins – they looked to me not much different from the Romanichals I knew. As I listened to them I suddenly realised that when they said *dzhoo-kool* this was our *jukel* (dog) – they were speaking *Romanes*! It was at this point that the reality of common ground amongst Romanies suddenly struck me, even though I could only follow a few isolated Romani words in their speech.

One unfortunate effect of Romani history was that Romanichals in the British Isles were, until recently, isolated from the mainstream of Romani life in Europe. Much of the Romanichals' knowledge about 'foreign' Romanies came not from their own direct knowledge and experience but from *gadžo* stereotypes and work of fiction. Romanichals, just like European Romanies, have also suffered the negative experiences of stereotyping, of misleading 'gypsy' images, exclusion, marginalisation, harassment, discrimination and overt antigypsyism. In spite of this, Romanichals often saw 'foreign' Romanies as strange, different, somehow separate and viewed them with suspicion. Thankfully, this *gadžo*-induced artificial isolation and suspicion has begun to break down over the last thirty years. Ian Hancock's book will go a long way to further breaking down this suspicion and clearing up misconceptions amongst Romanies themselves. It will foster a sense of unity amongst Romanies that is essential in a Europe that now includes the United Kingdom, a Europe that is grappling with pressing social problems amongst Romanies.

In 1969 my parents travelled from England to India, retracing the migration path of our people. An account of that wonderful and unique journey was recorded in the book *Gypsies – Wanderers of the World* (by Bart McDowell, National Geographic Publications, Washington, 1972). On that trip, my parents met many different Romanies in many different lands. And in each country they had been to, they were able to find at least a few Romani words in common with the local Romanies, confirming the view that there was commonality amongst all of us. After leaving India they came to Australia, recounting stories, showing me photographs, playing records of Romani music they had bought. They also told me of the many Romanies they had met and how they had been able to use the Romani language. They told me how some of the European Romanies were beginning to struggle for Romani rights in Europe. Shortly after, I heard of the first tentative steps towards Romani solidarity through the First World Romani Congress in 1971 in London.

In my years in Australia, I have met many of our people, *Romanichals* and Greek, Macedonian, Yugoslavian and Spanish Romanies – and lately

Romanian, Czech and Bulgarian. But we were all foreign Romanies in a foreign land, peopled by *gadže*.

All of these things convinced me of the essential unity of the diverse Romani people. And in this book, Professor Ian Hancock has provided further proof of the truth of that phrase – *Unity in Diversity*.

Professor Hancock is well known both as a distinguished scholar and as a pioneering Romani author, forcefully presenting a Romani voice and challenging the dominance of *gadže* in Romani studies. He continues this advocacy role in this work. He has distilled his years of experience as a Romani, as an academic and as a tireless political activist and packed them into a concise yet authoritative introduction to the diversity of Romani life and culture. Although he mainly looks at one of the largest Romani language groups in Europe and the world – the speakers of Vlax dialects – he covers many other aspects of Romani life.

He discusses Romani history, from the original migrations out of India to refugee flows at the present time. He also deals with the strong cultural retentions from India within Romani life and also provides information on the latest genetic researches that confirm the Romani origin in India.

He provides details not only of the migratory movements of Romani groups, but also of the reasons why shifts of population have occurred. Throughout the first part of the book, Ian Hancock introduces details of Romani culture, customs and rituals that illustrate both the variety and the commonality of Romani life. He also provides a chapter on various aspects of different Romani cuisines and on our Romani beliefs about health and illness. He stresses how these two things are linked in the Romani way of life. And in the final chapter of the book, he reveals his skills and training as a linguist, discussing our Romani language and providing a selection of proverbs that illustrate Romani life.

Professor Hancock also exposes the dark side of Romani history. He examines the centuries of slavery in Romania and the terrible and continuing impact this has had on many Romani people. He also points out that Romani slavery and enforced labour occurred in other parts of the world. He examines the attempted Romani genocide under the Nazis, which, like the experience of slavery, continues to affect the lives of Romanies today. He also provides a detailed discussion of the causes of antigypsyism, in particular the role of stereotypical images of 'The Gypsies'.

On a more positive note, Professor Hancock provides valuable advice

on how *gadže* could become more sensitive in interacting with Romanies, advice that will make the task of understanding Romani culture
much easier. He also gives a concise summary of the emergence of
Romani politics – although he modestly plays down his own significant
contribution in this area. Again on a positive note, he surveys a number
of famous Romani people in different walks of life. Most important, he
concludes the book by suggesting further readings, including several
valuable Romani websites.

Ian Hancock descends on his father's side from the family of Benczi
Imre, which left Hungary from the region of Einser, between Mosonmag-
yarovar and the Austrian border, in the second half of the nineteenth century during a large migration that brought Romungre Romanies both to
western Europe and to the United States. One of Benczi Imre's two
daughters, Maria, married into the British West Country showman family
of Hancock, and had three children, among them Marko who married
Gertrude, a daughter of the Romanichal King family. One of their children was Reginald ("Redjo"), Ian Hancock's father, who married Kitty, a
daughter of Arthur ("Jack") Palmer, who was a Romanichal scrap mer-
chant and locally-reputed boxer in the south-east of England in the
1920s. In the late 1950s he went to Canada but returned to England in
1961, and without finishing his high-school education obtained work in
various factories in west London as a spray painter. He lived at that time
in a rooming-house mainly occupied by students from Sierra Leone,
West Africa, and in their company he was able to learn Krio, the principal language of their country. Because of his success in collecting its
vocabulary, and through academic connections within that community,
he came to the attention of Professor David Dalby at the University of
London, who made it possible for him to enter the doctoral program at
that institution; the British Prime Minister at that time was Harold
Wilson, whose short-lived affirmative action program made provision for
special minority cases to receive higher education, and Hancock, along
with just one other person, qualified; possessing neither a high school
diploma, a BA nor an MA, he received his PhD degree from London
University in 1971 and is today the author of over 300 articles and books,
mostly on aspects of Romani history, human rights and culture. He
became active in the Romani movement in the late 1960s. Further details
about Professor Hancock's life and family can be found in Eliott Barkan
(ed.) *They Made it in America: Prominent Ethnic Americans* (New York:

ABC-CLIO, 2001), in Billy Cribb's *Tarmac Warrior* (London: Main-stream Publishing, 2001), in *Lacio Drom* No. 6 (1985) and in *Džaniben* No. 3 (1996).

In 1997 he accepted the international Rafto Foundation Human Rights Prize in Norway for his work, and in the same year was awarded the Gamaliel Chair in Peace and Justice at the University of Wisconsin. In 1998 the then President of the United States Bill Clinton (himself of Romani descent, see p. 130) appointed him to represent Romanies on the U S Holocaust Memorial Council. Until 2000 he represented the International Romani Union on the Economic and Social Council of the United Nations and in UNICEF. He teaches Romani Studies at The University of Texas in Austin, where he is Director of The Romani Archives and Documentation Center.

Written specifically as a handbook for schoolteachers, social workers, physicians and others in Central and Eastern Europe who interact professionally with Romanies, Professor Hancock's introduction to Romani life and customs will do two things. For *gadže*, it will clear up misconceptions, challenge stereotypes and replace misinformation with fact, and thus lay the foundations for a better understanding and tolerance between *gadže* and Romanies. It will also lay the foundations for a better understanding and tolerance between different Romani groups by highlighting the essential unity of our people, looking at our common experiences rather than our differences.

Ken Lee, Ph.D.
Lecturer in Sociology and Anthropology
Faculty of Education and Arts
University of Newcastle
New South Wales, Australia

Anglune Lava

Jorge M. Fernández Bernal

Growing up as a Rrom is now – and always was – difficult; the racism, hatred, violence, prejudices and discrimination that we face in daily life in some of the countries of this beautiful planet where we live, often do not allow us to enjoy the good life that all human beings deserve.

I grew up as a Vlax-speaking Rrom in Argentina, South America, where I too faced the discrimination and the prejudices of others, especially at school due to the difference of language and all the false ideas the non-Romanies had about our people. My country and its inhabitants shared the same prejudices as their ancestors in Europe who had conquered these lands where I live, and our elders who came from Russia, Greece or Serbia, knowing this, taught us that getting on with outsiders was not at all easy. For that reason we learned to keep our origins a secret, saying that we were of Greek or Italian descent, and that our language was Ancient Greek, etc., even though at the same time being proud of what we are, Rrom, but many times fearing to openly admit our identity, origin and culture, especially in our dealings with institutions and those in authority.

In the early 1980s I received a letter from Professor Ian Hancock. Who was this man who showed me a totally different world of which I could be even prouder? There in my hands through his letters an entirely new world was appearing, the origin of our culture, traditions, language, the clues to our Indian origin and many other things, none of which were taught us by the *gadže*. It encouraged me to continue working on our tales, language and, later, politics and in searching for our destiny, something that I had started some four or five years before that first letter, when I was a teenager who loved his own culture but was for some reason afraid of the outsider's world.

Time went by and we met each other, became friends and colleagues; sharing as our main aim in life a common love of our culture and our hope for its future.

In this admirable book Professor Hancock, for us "o Yanko le Redjosko", depicts the true Romani life, our traditions, origins, food, health care, language, etc., a really accurate description of all the so called 'mysteries' that surround our life.

Congratulations Professor Hancock, Phrala Yanko. I recommend this book to all those who feel sincerely attracted to our people. Newcomers as well as scholars will find it a good source of first-hand information from one of our people. Good reading!

Jorge Bernal
Writer and founder member of
The Council of the Organisations and Kumpanias of the Americas
(SKOKRA)

Introduction

Everywhere in Europe, throughout North and South America and in Australia, as well as in parts of Africa and Asia, there are found people who refer to themselves as Romani, and who maintain a language and a culture which set them quite apart from the rest of the world.

While this scattered population, which numbers about 12 million worldwide, calls itself *Romani*, the people among whom it lives refer to it by a great many other names: 'Gypsies', 'Zigeuner', 'Gitanos', 'Heiden', 'Cigani' and so on. And though everybody knows the 'Gypsies', far fewer really know the Romanies. Here are a people with two identities – their own actual Romani identity and the one that is familiar to most non-Romanies and which is reflected by those many other names.

Although we Romanies have lived in Europe for hundreds of years, almost all popular knowledge about us comes not from socializing with our people at first hand, for we generally live apart from the rest of the population, but from the way we are depicted in stories and songs and in the media. Such classic novels as *The Hunchback of Notre Dame* or *Wuthering Heights*, and stage plays, operas and films such as *Carmen* or *Der Zigeunerbaron* help to create an image which is romantic, perhaps, or sometimes scary, but not especially accurate. This book will talk about where that 'Gypsy' image originated, and what the Romani people are really like and how you can get to know more about us and our culture, history, feelings and aspirations. Throughout, the word *Romani* (plural *Romanies*) will be used to emphasize that other depictions with other names are misleading, and sometimes even harmful.

A note on Romani spelling

The spelling of Romani in this book is that found in Hancock (1985). Note that **c** by itself sounds like 'ts' in *cats*, **č** and **tj** both sound like the 'ch' in *choose*, **š**, and **ž** represent the sounds of 'sh' and 'zh' in *shoes* and *pleasure* respectively, **j** sounds like the English 'y', **dj** is the sound of 'j' in *jump*, **rr** is an 'r' pronounced in the throat as in French or German, **x** is like the German 'ch' in *Achtung* and **čh** and **dž** are like **č** and **ž** but with the tongue curled back towards the roof of the mouth. Unless otherwise indicated, all instances of Romani in the present work are in the Vlax dialect.

Some of the words in Chapter 2 are Romanian, not Romani, and are written in the orthography of that language. While Romani is Indic, Romanian is a romance language which descends from Latin and quite distinct from it. In Romanian, a *c* and a *g* before *e* or *i* sound like 'ch' in *choose* and 'g' in *giant* respectively, while *ch* and *gh* before *e* and *i* are like 'k' and 'g'. An **s** with a hook, **ş**, sounds like 'sh' in *shoes* and a **t** with a hook, **ţ**, is like 'ts' in *cats*. A *j* is like the 'zh' in *pleasure* (for example *ciocoi*, **Balş, vrăjitoari** and *ţigan* would sound like "chock-oy", "Balsh", "vruh-zhit-wari" and "tsigan" and would be spelt *čokoj, Balš, vrežitvari* and *cigan* if they were Romani words).

A note on names

In this book, except in quotes from other authors and where relevant to the discussion, the word *Gypsy* is not used. There are two reasons for this: first, it is a name created by outsiders and is based upon a mistaken assumption about our true identity: we are not Egyptians. Second, it, and its equivalents in other languages, immediately brings to mind an inaccurate and sometimes negative image originating in works of literature. It isn't well liked by most Romanies in any case; indeed, over a century and a half ago James Crabb observed that "it is a fact not unworthy of a place in these remarks on the origin of this people, that they do not like to be called *gipsies*" (1832:21). One purpose of this book is to deconstruct the stereotype of fictional 'gypsies' and to replace it with a picture of the real population – the Romanies; therefore Romani will be used throughout as the overall name for our people. Nevertheless, the word 'Gypsy' continues to be used, and the transition to 'Roma(nies)' is a slow one. Writers

might help the process along by including a sentence such as "Romanies, popularly though inaccurately called Gypsies …" (rather than, for instance, "Gypsies, who prefer to be called Romanies …") in their text.

These two young Romani children, one from Hungary and one from Britain, reflect the wide range of physical type among our population.

While in the past few years the term *Roma* has gained increasing currency as a cover term for all populations which speak, or at some time in the past spoke, the Romani language, and while its use in this way is sanctioned by different Romani organizations (such as *e.g.* the Nordic Roma Council, Sa-Roma, Inc. and the Roma National Congress), not all groups accept it by any means. This is because the word *Rom* originally meant 'married Romani male', but after arrival in Europe, it diverged in two directions. For some it kept this interpretation but restricted it so that it applied to themselves and no one else, while for others, it came to mean only 'husband'. Thus the Sinti, for example, or the Romanichals or the Manush use the word only with this narrower meaning, and not as a self-ascription for their entire group. On the other hand, *all* groups use the adjective *Romani* to describe themselves. A Sinto or a Romanichal will readily admit to being a Romani person, to speaking the Romani language, and maintaining Romani culture. Therefore, following the common practice of using adjectival forms as nouns (*e.g.* she is a Bulgarian, he is a Hungarian), use of *Romani* (plural *Romanies*) will also be used in this way, as it has been in Britain for some time. In 2000 the Congress of the United States agreed to follow this practice; as of November that year, the Library of Congress has officially changed its subject heading from 'Gypsies' to 'Romanies'. In addition, the proper use of *Roma*, which is actually only a plural masculine noun, evidently confuses many journalists, who sometimes use it incorrectly as a singular noun, or even as an adjective ('she is a Roma', 'the Roma language'). Sometimes, *Romanes* is used in English as an alternative name for the language, Romani, and this should be avoided too. It is the correct form in Romani itself, but here it is an adverb, meaning 'Romanily' or 'in the Romani manner', and 'do you speak Romani' is asked *Vrakeres Rromanes?*, literally "Do you speak in the Romani way?". You could just as well say *hurjade-pen Rromanes* 'they dressed in the Romani manner' or *kiravel Rromanes* 'she's cooking in the Romani way'.

There are Romanies everywhere, even in China and Singapore, Australia and Africa, but by far the greatest number live in Europe and in North and South America. We are not a single homogeneous population and outwardly differ considerably from place to place; 'Gitanos' in Spain seem to have little in common with 'Gypsies' in England or with 'Tattare' in Sweden or 'Tsigani' in Romania. Yet we all call ourselves Romani, we all maintain aspects of the same culture and speak (or once spoke) dialects of the same original language and we all share some of the same genetic material in our biological makeup. Despite this, any sense of having once been a single people has long been lost, the common factor now being an awareness not of what we *are*, but of what all of us are *not*: Romanies are not *gadže* or non-Romani people.

Put another way, from this point of view all of us divide the world into people who are *gadže* and people who are not, and while the different groups of people who are *not* each call themselves Romani, that label is not regarded as being all-inclusive: two different Romani groups may each deny that the other are 'true' Romanies. This is the result of several factors: long separation over time and distance, use of a different dialect of Romani or not speaking Romani at all, different historical or contemporary occupations, greater 'mixture' with non-Romani people, and so on. The same attitudes are found in other *gadžikane* populations too, but it's no wonder that determining who and what we are can be confusing to the outside world! Only now are Romani activists trying to instill a sense of historical unity among the different groups but so far this is proving very difficult to achieve.

Gipsy, Gypsy, Romany, Romani and Rromani

The word *Gipsy/Gypsy* derives from the word 'Egyptian', which was written in various ways during the sixteenth and seventeenth centuries: *Egipcian, Egypcian, 'gipcian, 'gypcian*. It was from the spellings which had lost the initial capital *E* that the word 'gypsy' comes, and this is one reason why it is so often spelt with a minuscule (lower case) initial letter. This is especially significant in English, which writes proper nouns with capital initial letters, and writing 'Gypsy' as 'gypsy' has only reinforced the common idea that we are a people defined by behaviour rather than by ethnicity.

Spelling 'Gipsy' with an 'i' is rare these days. The very first organization devoted to the study of our people, the Gypsy Lore Society, which was created in 1888, chose the spelling with 'y', and this has become the most common, although as has been emphasized in this book, the word is being increasingly rejected altogether in favour of *Roma(ni)*.

Romani is sometimes written *Romany*. This was a spelling popularized by the nineteenth century British writer George Borrow (who at first spelt it *Rommany*). Writing it with a final 'i' seems also to have been first introduced into English by the Gypsy Lore Society, which was probably simply adopting the spelling already being used by German, French and other Continental scholars. While a final 'y' ('*Romany*') remains common especially in works of fiction, it is increasingly seen as rather old fashioned. The United Nations, the Council of Europe, the U S Library of Congress as well as Romani organizations themselves (with the exception of one or two in Britain) have all adopted the spelling *Romani*. Nevertheless, all four of these spellings are found in the English-language literature, and this should be kept in mind when doing word-searches for Romani-related materials on the Web. Note too that the recommended pronunciation is to rhyme the word with *hominy*, with the stress on the first syllable, and the 'o' as in 'hot' rather than as in 'roam' or 'Rome'.

Sometimes, *Rom* and *Romani* are spelt with a double *R*, thus *Rrom, Rromani*. This is becoming well established in Romani itself since it represents a sound different from the one written with a single *R*: *raj* (gentleman) and *rraj* (twig) or *čorimos* (theft) and *čorrimos* (poverty) are different words which are pronounced differently, and therefore they need to be spelt differently. There have been different attempts to represent the /rr/ sound, *e.g.* 'ɽ' and 'ř', but use of the double-*R* has had the most success, probably because it does not require any accent marks. Its use in other languages, however, is not so common. The Romanian government supports it because it helps distinguish *Rromani* from *Romania,* but it is too soon to know whether it will gain wide currency elsewhere.

'Gadže' and other words for non-Romanies

The commonest word in our language for all non-Romani people is *gadže*, singular *gadžo*, though there are several others. It is not a proper noun, nor is it an offensive word; it simply means 'non-Romani people'. The often-encountered *gorgio* (another spelling which is a legacy from George Borrow) is the same word in the Romanichal (English Romani) dialect. Preferred spellings for *gorgio* are *gaujo*, *gawjo* or *gawja*, which better represent its pronunciation.

Nineteenth century English-language treatments of Romanies sometimes used the word *gentiles* to designate non-Romani people. This was in part stimulated by the excessive missionary activity among Romanies in Britain at that time, contrasting and emphasizing our 'un-Christian' ways, and in part due to the frequent association of Romanies with the Jewish people. The term is seldom used today in this context (though *cf.* Matras, 1998:8 and Nemeth 2002:70) and its continued use is not recommended; after all, Hindus, Jews and Muslims are all *gadže* too.

Questions

1   Why haven't Romanies ever been called by their real name?
2   Why does there seem to be no sense of group unity among Romanies, compared with other diaspora populations such as the Armenians or Jews?
3   To what extent does this characteristic underlie the present-day problems of Romanies?

CHAPTER ONE

History

No nation knows itself until it knows its past

Ben Ames Williams

Romanies first arrived in Europe at the end of the thirteenth century, at a time when the Ottoman Turks were taking over the Christian Byzantine Empire in order to spread the Muslim religion and extend their political influence. At first, some Europeans thought that the Romanies were Turks too and, in some places, that is still a name applied to us; another name reflecting this mistaken idea was *Saracen*, which is what the French and German people called us. The non-Christian association is evident in an early Dutch name, *Heiden* ('heathens'). But there were two names in particular which stuck, and which have lasted to this day, both of them also based on mistaken identity: 'Tsingani' and 'Egyptian'. The first, Tsingani, which has produced such forms as *Cingano, Cikan, Zigeuner* and *Çingene*, is from Byzantine Greek *Ατσίγγανοι* (pronounced 'atsingani'), a name given to Romanies during the Byzantine period and which means something like the 'don't touch' or 'hands off' people. Because Romanies were seen to keep a distance from everyone else, they were given this nickname. The other label, 'Egyptian', has become even more widespread, as *Gypsy, Sipsiwn, Ijito, Gjupci, Gitano, Yiftos, Gitan* and so on.

There are several explanations for this association with Egypt: firstly that the mediaeval Europeans used 'Egyptian' indiscriminately as a cover-term for a number of different foreign populations at that time; secondly, that upon arrival in Europe, Romanies stayed for a while in a place on the Adriatic coast known as 'Little Egypt' and thirdly, that some actually did call themselves Egyptians. There is some evidence that numbers of Romanies at that early period had been forcibly removed from the Balkans to Egypt by the Ottomans but managed to make their way back to Europe, and then said they had come there from that country (Ken Lee, 2001). Nevertheless, the name 'Egyptians' ('Αιγύπτιοι), probably first used to refer to Domaris then later to Romanies, was already being used in the Byzantine Empire before their move on into Europe, and so may have been brought in from there (Soulis, 1961:148). In Hungary, Romania and Russia, Romanies were also referred to as 'pharaoh's people'. The one name that the Europeans *didn't* use for the newcomers was *Roma*. And while some of the first to arrive in the West told people where they had originally come from – India – this never became common knowledge. It was not until four and a half centuries later that European scholars began to learn who we really were.

How Westerners learnt the Romanies' true origin

The way that the connection between Romanies and India came to be known was something of an accident. It happened in 1760, in Holland. There, a theology student from western Hungary named Vályi Stefán was sitting one day in the common room at the University of Leiden with three exchange students from Malabar in India, who were discussing the ancient Indian language, Sanskrit. Vályi's family owned a large estate in the town of Győr, where many Romanies were employed as labourers. Vályi had befriended some of them and had learnt a few words and phrases of our language. When he heard the Indian students using Sanskrit words, he recognised some similarities with Romani. He wasn't a language specialist and wasn't sure what to do with this new-found information, but he mentioned it to an acquaintance – a printer named Nemeth Istvan – who, three years later, related the story to someone else, an army captain named Szekely von Doba who in turn told the story to yet another person, the scholar Georg Pray. Sixteen years after the event, and now at third-hand, Pray published an account of it in the *Vienna Gazette* in 1776. From that point on, different specialists such as Rüdiger (1782), Grellmann (1783), Marsden (1785) and others began to investigate further. Romani Studies had begun.

Once the language was recognised as Indian, right away many new questions arose. If Romanies spoke a language from India, the scholars

said, then they must themselves be Indian. Today, we would not make such an assumption so readily; there is no connection whatsoever between a person's genetic ancestry and the language he speaks, but people didn't understand that in 1800. And if they were Indian, they continued, then what are they doing in Europe? And why did they leave India, and when? And did they have a country, and were there still Romanies living there? Some of these questions have kept western scholars busy to this day, and we know a great deal more now than was understood two hundred years ago.

"Because of their strange dances, romantic songs and wandering life, Gypsies have always been thought of as mysterious and exciting". Text and illustration from *The Linkletter Picture Encyclopedia for Boys and Girls* (New York: Harwyn Publishing Corporation, 1961:132). The clothing depicted is not Romani, and showing the legs above the calves is taboo in Romani culture.

It is significant that, despite the growing body of academic support for an Indian origin for our people, other, more fantastic suggestions continued to be made into the nineteenth and twentieth centuries even after our Indian origin became incontrovertibly established – for example, that we were from the lost city of Atlantis, or (together with Native Americans, the Basques and the Bedouin people) descended from a prehistoric race of horsemen who

once rode all over the Earth. As if the true story of the Romani people
were not already fascinating enough, the compulsion of writers to make
us mysterious and otherworldly continues to this day. Walter Starkie, in
the introduction to a book on Romanies, wrote "there are over five million Gypsies wandering about the world today ... they are still as mysterious as when they entered Europe in the fifteenth century. Sprung from
Dravidian stock in the northwest of India, they were pariahs and, according to tradition metal workers, minstrels, story tellers and fakirs"
(1972:*i*). Even encyclopedias promote this 'strange' image; the eight-
volume *American Educator* for example has the following entry:

> GYPSIES, *jip'sis*, a group of strange people ... It is not known with cer-
> tainly where they first appeared, but a Hindu origin is probable ... Only
> instinct such as is found in the lower animals seems to lead them to follow
> in the path of their ancestors (Foster and Hughes, 1924:1603).

The first academic hypothesis, based on the newly learnt connection with
India, was that since Romanies in Europe were poor and did menial jobs,
and were often entertainers, then this must be how they lived before leaving their homeland. There, such a way of life describes members of the
Shudra caste, and thus it was proposed by Heinrich Grellmann in 1783
that we descend from this, the lowest social level in India. This system is
complex but, broadly speaking, it divides all of Hindu society into four
castes (*varnas*) and hundreds of sub-castes or social tiers (*jatis*), with the
Brahmins or holy men at the top, the *Kshatriyas* or warriors occupying
the second highest place, the *Vaisyas* or merchants and producers on the
third level, and the *Shudras* at the bottom; and outside the structure altogether are the out-caste populations. Members of the three highest
castes claim descent from the people calling themselves Aryan (Kumar,
2001:1-2), while the Shudra caste was composed of indigenous people of
mostly Dravidian and Munda descent. Of course in real life Indian society is not neatly compartmentalized like this, and there are people of
Dravidian descent who are Brahmins, and the so-called Aryan population
is clearly very much intermarried with the the non-Aryan people of India.
The idea of an 'Aryan' identity has no scientific basis in any case, but the
belief that it does has had deadly consequences for our people, which are
discussed in Chapter 4.

In 1830, a British army officer in India named James Harriott published part of a story found in the Persian *Book of Kings* (the *Shah*

Nameh) that was written by the poet Firdausi in the eleventh century. The story relates an incident that took place in the fifth century, when the Indian King Shankal made a gift of 12,000 musicians to his son-in-law, Bahram Gur, who was the Shah of Persia at that time. This no doubt happened, since the same story has been recorded independently by other writers too. Harriott suggested that those musicians were the ancestors of the Romanies since, as the story continues, after a year they were sent away by Bahram Gur and presumably moved westwards towards Europe. This theory was immediately seized upon by the scholars of the day because it provided an explanation as to why a large group of Indians, and particularly musicians, left India and apparently kept on travelling. Today, over 170 years since it was first proposed, this account of Romani origins is still being repeated in the very latest publications (for example di Renzo 2001 or Altinoz 2001) – but as we shall see, it is wrong.

The next milestone in Romani Studies came in the 1840s when a scholar named Augustus Pott (1844) published an important two-volume work on the language. He included in it a copy of a letter he had received from a man named Brockhaus, who suggested that since Romanies called themselves *Rom*, this might be the same as the Indian word *Dom*, and since the Dom did menial jobs in India, just as the Romanies did in Europe, they were probably one and the same people.

About that time, it was learnt that there was another population that spoke an Indian language which lived in the Middle East, and which called itself *Dom* or *Domari*. This seemed to settle the matter: here must be the descendants of Bahram Gur's musicians, still living in Syria, Jordan, Jerusalem and elsewhere and still calling themselves by the original name. Later in the nineteenth century, European scholars learnt of yet another population speaking a language full of Indian words, this time in Armenia, and calling itself *Lom*. All three groups, Rom, Dom and Lom, were referred to as 'Gypsies' in the literature and all were assumed to have emerged from the same original migration out of India.

The details of this were published by the British romanologist John Sampson in 1923. He believed that the migration left India as one in the tenth century but having passed through Persia, it separated into three groups, the first (the *Dom*) remaining in the Near East, the second (the *Lom*) branching off towards Armenia and the third (the *Rom*) continuing into Europe through Anatolia. In addition, Sampson was particularly interested in the relationship between Romani and the languages of India, and maintained that it was most closely connected to those spoken in the north-west, such as Sindhi or Multani. He was challenged in 1927 by another linguist, Turner, who said that Romani was more like the Central Indian languages, such as Hindi and Panjabi. Both Sampson and Turner, as well as others who have followed them, have reached some faulty conclusions because in their historical and comparative work, they examined Romani, Domari (the language of the Doms) and Lomavren (the language of the Loms) all together, on the assumption that their speakers simply represent branches of one original migration and, therefore, descend from one original language. We no longer think that this was the case. It also now seems that there are several populations similar to the Dom throughout the Middle East, and that they represent separate migrations of groups originally from India, who left at quite different times and under quite different circumstances, and who cannot be considered any closer to the Romani people than groups still in India, such as Panjabis or Gujaratis.

O Teljaripe: **The move out of India**

In the light of recent research into the origins of Romanies and the Romani language, particularly since Indian scholars have themselves begun to contribute to the discussion, a different picture has started to emerge. First of all, while the event that Firdausi related in the *Book of Kings* no doubt took place, and while the Doms in the Middle East may even descend from those musicians, an examination of their language makes it quite clear that it had a separate origin in India from Romani. Its grammar and the Indian words in it don't sufficiently match their equivalents in Romani in terms of their identification with specific areas and languages in India. Second, if Romani and Domari had parted company after having already passed through Persia, then the significant numbers of words from Persian which both languages have adopted should be the same, but they aren't. Most persuasive of all, in the fifth century, the languages of India had three grammatical genders for their nouns: masculine, feminine and neuter, just as in modern Czech or German or Bulgarian (for example, in Bulgarian you would say *мой* учител, *моя* стая and *мое* писмо – 'my teacher', 'my room', 'my letter;' in German you would say '*der* Mann, *die* Frau, *das* Mädchen 'the man', 'the woman', 'the girl'). In the New Indo-Aryan period, which began about

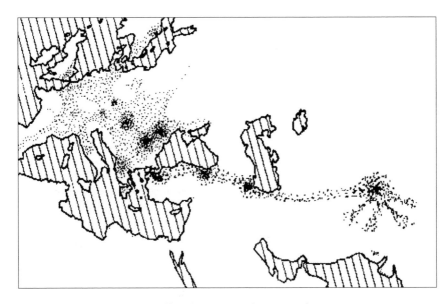

1000 AD, most of the Indian languages began to lose the neuter gender, leaving only two: masculine and feminine. Domari has evidence of three, showing that it must have been taken out of India when the languages there still had the third gender; but Romani has only two and, what is more, its nouns that were originally neuter have virtually all become new masculine nouns in Romani just as they have in Hindi and other languages still spoken in India. We can only conclude from this that at the time when the neuter began to disappear, around the year 1000, the ancestor languages that were to become Romani had not yet left their homeland. If the first possible account of the Romani presence in the western Byzantine Empire is in *The Life of St George the Athonite* which was written in 1068, then the window of time between the ancestors of the Romanies' leaving India and their arriving at the gates of Europe would have been fifty years or less; this would also explain why there was insufficient time to adopt any Arabic words into the language. That account, however, may be referring to the Domaris rather than to Romanies – their presence in the area (as "Lors", i.e. Luris) is recorded from the mediaeval period (Soulis, 1961:148-9).

Route of the migration from the Hindu Kush to Europe.

The second account, which Fraser (1992:46) says "clearly" refers to Romanies and in which they are called *Athinganoi* is found in a commentary by one Theodore Balsamon, who died *ca.* 1204, written towards the end of the twelfth century (Soulis, 1961:146). If it were the Seljuks, a Ghuzz Turkic people, who were instrumental in bringing the ancestors of the Romanies from Ghaznavid territory to Anatolia when they defeated the Armenians at Manzikert in 1071, then this second and more reliable account of Romanies in Constantinople would better match the time sequence. Soulis (1961:163) says

> We must conclude that the appearance of the Gypsies in Byzantine lands is undoubtedly connected with the Seljuk raids in Armenia where the Gypsies, who subsequently appeared in Europe, had stayed for a long time, as the great number of Armenian loanwords in their vocabulary testifies.

In 1038–40, some three decades before taking over Armenia, the Seljuks had already defeated the Ghaznavid conquerors of the Rajputs at Nisha-pur (Neyshabur) in Khorasan – today a part of eastern Iran – and they brought captives into the Byzantine Empire from both India and Persia "usually in a military capacity" (see *http://www.ucalgary. ca/applied_history/tutor/oldwrld/armies/seljuk.html*). One might surmise that the Seljuks' captives were the Rajput prisoners of war taken from the defeated Ghaznavids who were using them as fighters. It may well have been those same raids on the Armenians, which took place before the migration had moved into the Byzantine Empire proper, which caused the group that later became the Lom to split off and become established further east. There are no Greek words at all in their speech, Lomavren, and practically none of its massive Armenian vocabulary turns up in Romani. It does share with it much of its Indian-derived vocabulary – though with sufficiently different selections to suggest that neither lan-guage had yet stabilized at so early a date.

There is also a tenuous Seljuk connection with our name *Rom*. If it were the case that Romanies (and the Romani language) did not fully come into existence until this period, then it might be that this was also when the self-designation *Rom* was acquired. The Seljuk sultanate, which by this time extended into most of what had earlier been Byzan-tine territory, was called *Rum*, and even the Byzantines called themselves *Romaivi*, reflecting their beginnings as the Eastern Roman Empire.

Just as Islam had spread eastwards into India, initiating the move of our ancestors out of that part of the world, Muslim expansion towards the West, particularly initiated by the Seljuk Turks, was also the primary reason why they moved into Europe.

Examination of the Romani language also provides us with the next piece of the puzzle. Having determined on the basis of its grammar that the separation from India took place no earlier than the year 1000 – a date we can further confirm by the New Indo-Aryan sound-changes that have taken place in its pronunciation – we can also find some clues in its vocabulary. Since it is an Indian language, it shares its earliest and most basic words with other languages in India: the Romani word *pani* meaning 'water' for example, is exactly the same in Hindi, Panjabi, Nepali, Bengali, Marathi, Sindhi, Gujarati and fifty other Indian languages.

More recent evidence is found in a report dated June 2001 from the Centre for Human Genetics at Edith Cowan University in Perth. It concludes that:

> Analysis of slow-evolving polymorphisms has identified a single paternal and a single maternal lineage of Indian origin shared by all groups (of Romanies tested …). These lineages belong to a small subset of the known genetic diversity of the Indian subcontinent. Thus, Roma descend from a small ancestral minority in the Indian subcontinent that has subsequently fractured into multiple population isolates within Europe (Kalaydjieva et al., 1999:15).

Considered together with the linguistic evidence, this is consistent with the notion of a population of closely related groups which shared the same genetic markers but which differed linguistically (like, for instance, speakers of Celtic and Romance languages). The serological analyses by the geneticist Vijender Bhalla had already identified "a common ethnic substratum" in India that Romanies share with "Jat Sikhs, Panjabi Hindus and Rajputs" (1992:331–32).

As the migration moved towards the northwest and on towards Europe, new words from other languages were picked up and added to the vocabulary and these help to provide a map of the route that was taken. The presence of many words adopted from Persian (for example, *baxt* 'luck') and some from Kurdish (*vurdon* 'waggon') show that the migration must have passed through Iran; Armenian and Greek words (such as *kočak* 'button' and *zumi* 'soup') show passage through what is now Turkey; Slavic and Romanian words (*dosta* 'enough' and *raxuni* 'smock') indicate a presence in the Balkans.

Words can be grouped into sets according to their related area of use – for example, all the words describing body parts or cooking or building, and this too can tell us something. Thus almost all of the words having to do with metalwork are from Greek, and this leads us to believe that blacksmithing was not a particular skill brought from India, because the basic vocabulary would otherwise be Indian; and it also tells us that metalworking as a profession was acquired in the Byzantine Empire or in Greece. By the same token, Romani does have a set of words having to do with warfare, and these *are* of Indian origin. The words for 'fight', and 'soldier', and 'sword', and 'spear', 'plunder' and 'battle-cry' as well as several others have been a part of the language from the very beginning. The different words too, which we use to refer to someone who is not Romani, such as *gadžo* or *das* or *goro* or *gomi* meant such things as 'civilian', or 'prisoner of war', or 'captive' in their original Indian forms.

Assuming that these clues point to some kind of early military association, the next step is to see if there was any military activity in northern India in the eleventh century, the date by which Romanies may already have arrived in Byzantium. We find right away that between 1000 and 1027, India suffered a series of invasions led by Mahmud of Ghazni, who was attempting to spread the Muslim religion. His followers, known as the Ghaznavids, wrought terrible destruction throughout the Hindu Shahi territory in the Hindu Kush in the north of India, particularly in the area around Peshawar south of the Karakoram, killing thousands of people, taking many more captive and destroying many holy places. The Indian response was to assemble armies to confront the Islamic troops, and during this period of Indian history there were many battles between the two sides. Although the Ghaznavids were defeated by the Seljuks they were successful in their intent to spread their faith, and Islam is today the principal religion throughout the area. Sometimes the Indians won and were able to drive the Muslim armies back through the Himalayan passes and out of India; more often than not, however, the Indian troops left through those passes as prisoners of war.

The Indian militia was composed principally of Rajputs, whose name means 'sons of princes'; and who had resisted Islam for centuries. Who they actually were has not yet been determined; Kulke and Rothermund (1998:110) wrote:

> The antecedents of the [Rajput] tribes are unknown … it is possible that some of these tribes came from Central Asia in the wake of the invasion of the Huns and became part of local tribes … in the year 747 … all Rajput

clans were purified and admitted to the status of Kshatriyas ... the constant division of Rajput tribes into small exogamous clans led to the development of a complicated network of martial alliances. This in turn produced a fusion of the leadership of the Rajputs and gave rise to a common Rajput culture which is still characteristic of Rajasthan today.

Today, descendants of the various Rajput tribes are found speaking languages as different as Oriya and Rajasthani, and just as Urdu grew out of a mixture of languages spoken on the battlefields (the name *Urdu*, of Turkish origin, means 'army camp', it is where the English word 'horde' comes from, and another name for it was *Ryekhta*, which is the Persian word for 'mixed'), so the languages which were to become Romani appear to have come together in the same way. It was probably during this early period that most of Romani's Persian words were also adopted just as they were by Urdu – over half of the *ca.*100 found in Romani are shared by both – since it was the language of administration and the militia, and widely spoken throughout the area; in fact, another early name for battlefield Urdu was "the Persic of Indostan". It is the case too that although their own language was Turkish, Persian was also the military language of the Seljuks, and it served as the lingua franca amongst the divers peoples whom they had captured to fight for them. Just one Seljuk (though originally Mongolian) word seems to have found its way into Romani: *mandjin* "treasure". This probably entered the language some time later than AD 1227, when the Seljuk-controlled Sultanate of Rum came under the temporary influence of the Kipchak Mongols.

In those days, armies were accompanied by large numbers of camp followers, whom the Indians called *shiviranuchara*. These were men and women whose jobs included clearing the battlefields, erecting tents, cooking for the soldiers and entertaining them, mending broken weapons and attending to the wounded. These people did not belong to the Kshatriya (warrior) caste, but together with the Rajputs, whether as prisoners of war or with victors routing the enemy, they left India through the Hindu Kush. Women were well represented among the camp followers, though they were not part of the military, and it is to this that the female Indian genome in the modern genetic makeup of the Romani population may be traced. The Cowan University study (Gresham et al., 2001) demonstrates more diversity in its female than in its male composition, and that subsequent rules of marriage appear to have been, and have

Roma-Banjara, published
in India, recognises the
historical link between
our two populations.

remained, more permissive of female than of male outsiders marrying into closed Romani society.

If they were not taken as a captive fighting force by the Seljuks and had left earlier routed by the Ghaznavids then, given their numbers and location, their route out was most probably via the Swat River Valley or the Kaghan Valley. From there they would have followed the Silk Road through Khorasan and continued south of the Caspian Sea and across the foothills of the Caucasus Mountains to Trebizond on the north coast of what is today Turkey. The Persian word that refers to the Caspian, *deryav*, the first massive body of water encountered by the migrants, gave Romani its word for 'sea:' *dorjavo*. The fact that there are also two Indian words for 'silk' in Romani, *phanrr* and *kež* may be historically relevant, since silk isn't a particularly significant item in Romani culture today.

Some ethnic groups in modern India claim descent from the Rajputs, including the Banjara (also called the Lobana or Ghor) whose own history, i.e. that numbers of their ancestors left India forever at the time of Ghaznavid invasions, supports what we are beginning to piece together about Romani history. Rathore (1998:2) gives the names of several Banjara and non-Banjara historians who have written about their own history, and about the Rajputs "who left Rajputana in response to the Ghaznavid invasions, spreading out to the four points of the compass". Twenty years before that Naik (1978:5) had already written of the Rajputs who "about 1,000 years ago, during the invasion of Mohammed Ghori and Mohammed Ghazni into Greater Panjab... fled through the Khyber and Bolan Passes and went into Central Asia". The Banjara recognise a relationship with Romanies, and sometimes attend Romani functions in Europe, and invite us to their own meetings in India.

There are other parallels between Rajput and Romani cultures. There are stories remembered by some Romani groups of our ancestors' having left their homeland because of a great conflict with Islam. These new linguistic and historical findings have been supported by recent work done by geneticists comparing Romani and Indian blood types. Bhalla (op cit, 331–32) concluded in his own study that Romanies are genetically most like the Rajput populations in India and least like the present-day Dom:

> The Rajputs occupy the position nearest the Gypsies. The dominant ethnic element in the Doms and Kolis [however] ... is not reflected in any sizeable proportion in the genetic makeup of East European Gypsies.

Indian scholars have observed that many aspects of Romani culture clearly parallel high-caste behaviour rather than low-caste, a further argument against the *dom* or low-caste origins hypothesis. Rishi believes that "the majority of Roma, before migrating from India, formed a vital part of the upper strata of the Indian population, like Rajputs or Kshatriyas or Jats" (1977:13); Kochanowski (1968:28) reached the same conclusion: "The more any [Indian] people resemble the high castes of Delhi, the Hindu Panjabis and Rajputs in general, the more they resemble the Romanies (the European Gypsies)". That the Dom or other migratory populations do not seem to have constituted the original population is further supported by an examination of the vocabulary; Kochanowski (1995:4) and Ronald Lee (2001:35) have both suggested that the presence of native Indian words in Romani for such concepts as 'king', 'house', 'door', 'sheep', 'pig', 'chicken', 'landowner' (*thagar, kher, vudar, bakro, balo, khaxni, raj*) and so on point to settled, rather than nomadic, peoples. To this it may be added that the words for 'tent', 'waggon', 'buffalo', 'set up camp', 'strike camp' and even 'road' are not of Indian origin. It also casts doubt upon *dom* as being the source of the word *Rrom*, for which other etymologies have been proposed (for example the Old Indo-Aryan *rāma* "husband", the meaning it retains in Romani itself).

O Aresipe: Arrival in Byzantium and the West

Perhaps as captives of the Seljuks, or perhaps travelling quickly to avoid the north-easterly spread of Islam and advancing in a series of confrontations with the non-Muslim Huns, the Romanies' move out of India and through the Middle East would seem to have taken place comparatively rapidly, in fifty years or less. If they had left as a defeated people rather than as victors, which seems the likelier case, then going back into India and the territories now occupied by Mahmud's armies would have been an unattractive option – and no option at all if they were prisoners of war. But if it took so little time to reach Anatolia, it was another two and a half centuries before the Romanies moved on into Europe. There are more than 250 Greek words in the European Romani dialects taken together,

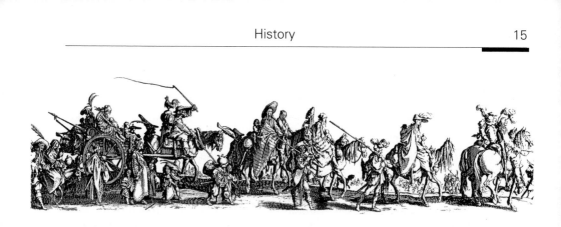

second only in number to the Indian vocabulary. There is
also some fundamental grammar of Greek origin; it was
probably in the Byzantine Empire that Romani finally
crystallized into the language we recognise today. This,

and other cultural characteristics point to a long and close contact with
the Byzantines. The time period too is supported in a little-known but
important paper by Fraser where he determined, applying the technique
of lexico-statistical dating to Romani, that "the lexical unity of Romani
in Europe began to break up [within the Byzantine Empire] about 1040
AD" (1989:14).

From 1071 onwards, the Byzantine Empire was gradually being occupied by the Muslims, whose territory continued to grow as they edged
closer and closer to Europe, until in 1453 Mohammed II defeated
Emperor Constantine and the city of Byzantium (then renamed Constantinople and now called Istanbul) fell to the Ottoman Turks. The earliest
accounts of a Romani presence at the gateway to the Balkans, however,
are from the late 1200s; there is a document from Constantinople dated
1283 referring to taxes collected from "the so-called Egyptians and
Tsigani".

Perhaps because of their original military training, Romanies were
conscripted into the Turkish battalions and many entered Europe that
way. By the 1300s, there were permanent Romani military settlements at
Nauplia and Modon, located on opposite sides of Peloponnesia in southern Greece. Marushiakova and Popov (1997:63) say:

> Without a doubt, many of the Romanies in the Balkans were carried
> thence along with the Ottoman invasion: either as direct participants,
> mainly as servants in the auxiliary detachments or as craftsmen servicing
> the army, or with the accompanying [Turkish] population.

The Romanies in Greece called themselves *Romiti*, probably a reference to their earlier home in the Sultanate of Rum. Whether they served the Turks willingly or not we don't know. Because they were not Muslims, their social status in the Ottoman Empire was not one of equals, and while some Romanies came in as attachments to the Turkish troops, others found a place in the economy as metal workers, carpenters or entertainers using skills acquired during the Greek Byzantine period. Yet still others were evidently brought in as slaves, as they may have already come into Europe with the Tatars even earlier. It was in the Ottoman-occupied Balkans, specifically in the principalities of Moldavia and Wallachia, that the enslavement of Romanies became established and lasted for over 500 years. The overall effect of this on the Romani people was devastating and turned a skilled, self-sufficient people into dependent, dispirited chattel (see Hancock, 1987).

Questions

1 How have genetics, history and linguistics worked together to help us reconstruct Romani origins and identity?
2 How was the Indian connection of the Romanies first recognised?
3 What incorrect assumptions were then made, and why?
4 Name some of the prominent figures in early Romani Studies. What were their contributions?
5 How can we be sure about the latest date that the ancestors of the Romanies must still have been in India?
6 What common factor caused the ancestors of the Romanies (a) to leave India and (b) to enter Europe?

CHAPTER TWO

Rrobija: Slavery

[After receiving the news that slavery had ended], for some minutes there was great rejoicing and thanksgiving, and wild scenes of ecstasy ... the wild rejoicing on the part of the emancipated coloured people lasted for but a brief period, for I noticed that by the time they returned to their cabins there was a change in their feelings. The great responsibility of being free, of having charge of themselves, of having to think and plan for themselves and their children, seemed to take possession of them. It was very much like suddenly turning a youth of ten or twelve years out into the world to provide for himself. In a few hours, the great questions with which the Anglo-Saxon race had been grappling for centuries had been thrown upon these people to be solved. These were the questions of a home, a living, the rearing of children, education, citizenship, and the establishment and support of churches. Was it any wonder that within a few hours, the wild rejoicing ceased and and a feeling of deep gloom seemed to pervade the slave quarters

(Washington, 1901:20–1).

Partly because of the draining effects of the Crusades in earlier centuries, Balkan society at the time of the arrival of the first Romanies was technologically backward and mainly agricultural but, as its peasant economy gradually shifted to a market-based one, it came to depend more and more upon the artisan skills that the Romanies were bringing with them. The Romanian peasantry, though not made slaves, was made into serfs (*krepostniči* or *jobagi* in Old Slavic) as this economic order began to to change.

Romanies, who at first had found work with the feudal landlords, became associated with particular estates and by the early 1300s were being included in parcels of property given as gifts or as payment by one

A *şatra* or slave settlement,
Wallachia, 1862

owner to another, as well as to the monasteries; the
earliest written evidence of this refers to such tributes
being made even before 1350. But slavery as we think
of it today, called *robie* in Romanian, emerged later
out of the increasingly strict measures taken by the landowners, the aristocracy and the monasteries to prevent their Romani labour force from
leaving the principalities, which is what was beginning to happen
because of the greater and greater demands being placed upon them as a
work force. Those who owned slaves were protected by legislation – the
rept ţigan or 'rights (over) Romanies' – that gave them complete control
over every aspect of their lives.

The Romanies' status as slaves, and as foreigners and non-Muslims,
gave them scant legal redress. According to the Islamic world-view of the
occupying Ottomans, it was entirely acceptable to treat any conquered,
non-Muslim population as property, and by the 1500s the word *ţigan* had
come specifically to mean 'Romani slave'.

Other words for 'slave' were *rob* (plural *robili*), *sclav* and *scindrom*;
they were broadly divided into field slaves (*ţiganii de ogor*) and house
slaves (*ţiganii de casaţi*, *ţiganii vatraşi* or *ţiganii de vatra*), the latter further divided into two groups, (1) slaves of the Crown or state, namely
those of the noblemen (the *sclavi domneşti*), the court (*sclavi curte*) and
the householders (*sclavi gospod*), and (2) the slaves of the Church (the

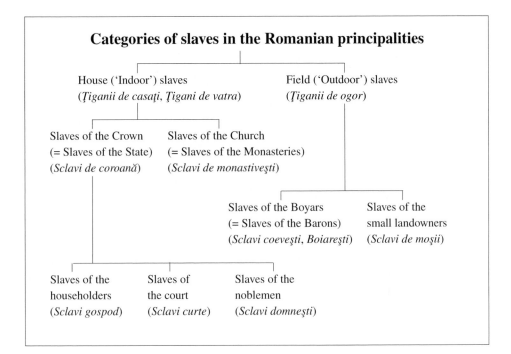

Categories of slaves in the Romanian principalities

House ('Indoor') slaves
(*Ţiganii de casaţi, Ţigani de vatra*)

Field ('Outdoor') slaves
(*Ţiganii de ogor*)

Slaves of the Crown
(= Slaves of the State)
(*Sclavi de coroană*)

Slaves of the Church
(= Slaves of the Monasteries)
(*Sclavi de monastiveşti*)

Slaves of the Boyars
(= Slaves of the Barons)
(*Sclavi coeveşti, Boiareşti*)

Slaves of the
small landowners
(*Sclavi de moşii*)

Slaves of the
householders
(*Sclavi gospod*)

Slaves of
the court
(*Sclavi curte*)

Slaves of the
noblemen
(*Sclavi domneşti*)

Various occupations of the slaves

Goldwasher (*Aurari, Rudari, Zlatari*)
Charcoal-burner (*Cărbunari*)
Maker of bowls, troughs, etc. (*Blidari*)
Flower-seller (*Vînzători*)
Basket-maker (*Chirpaci*)
Fortune-teller (*Vrăjitoari*)
Sieve-maker (*Ciurari*)
Blacksmith (*Covaci, Ferari, Potcovari*)
Handyman (*Laieţi*)
Seamstress (*Cusătoreaşă*)
Hut-builder (*Salahori*)
Torturer (*Torturari*)
Fisherman (*Pescari*)

Bear-trainer (*Ursari, Rič̆hinari*)
Spoon-carver (*Lingurari*)
Metal-worker (*Costărari*)
Cauldron-maker (*Călderari*)
Whitewasher (*Spoitoresari*)
Whitewash brush-maker (*Chivuşari*)
Knife-grinder (*Ascuţitoari*)
Locksmith (*Lăcătuş*)
Violin-player (*Lăutari*)
Cook (*Bucătăreasă*)
Laundryman (*Spălători*)
Boot-mender (*Cioabători*)
Executioner (*Îndeplinari*)

etc.

A *şatra*, Wallachia, 1862

sclavi monastiveşti). The field slaves were likewise divided into two groups, those of the *boyars* or land-barons, called the *sclavi coeveşti* or *sclavi boiereşti* and those of the small landowners, the *sclavi de moşii*. The slaves of the Crown had three principal occupations: goldwasher, bear-trainer and spoon-maker. In addition, there were slaves known as *laieşi* who were allowed to move about the estates doing a variety of jobs, including those of musician, farrier, whitewasher, sieve-maker, blacksmith and copper-smith – this last occupation has given its name to the biggest single Romani group of all, the Kalderash. Slaves of the Church were grooms, cooks and coachmen; among the house slaves were *scopiţi*, males castrated so as not to present a threat to the noblewomen whom they served.

Field slaves lived in *şatras* or collections of reed and mud huts on the outskirts of the estates that were seldom visited by their owners. They were not allowed to have musical instruments for their own amusement and they were bought and sold in lots, also called *şatras*, *cetas* or *salaşes*. Groups of slaves remained under the supervision of a *vatav* or overseer (also called a *ciocoi*) who was sometimes brutally cruel; and although it was forbidden by law to kill a slave, that was not an infrequent occurrence. House slaves were not allowed to speak Romani, and their descendants, the *Boyash* (also written *Beyash* or *Bayash* – from *boiar* "land baron") today have a variety of the Latin-based Romanian, rather than Romani, as their mother tongue. Female house slaves were also given to visitors for entertainment; the mixed children resulting from this abuse automatically became slaves. In the sixteenth century, a Romani child could be purchased for the equivalent of 48 cents (32p). By the nineteenth century, slaves were sold by weight, at the rate of one gold piece per pound. Punishments for the slaves included flogging, the *falague* (shredding the soles of the feet with a whip), cutting off the lips, burning with lye, being thrown naked into the snow, hanging over smoking fires and wearing a three-cornered spiked iron collar called a *cangue*. Slaves were sometimes able to escape and take refuge in communities in the Carpathian Mountains; those people are called *netoţi* in the literature (the plural of *netoto*) but there is no trace of their descendants today. Some of them must have originated from the steady trickle of slaves escaping during the 1700s when the

Vlad Tepov, "Vlad the Impaler", who delighted in torturing his Romani victims.

demand for their labour had once again become intolerable, a direct response to the principalities' new role as a supplier of grain to major western European markets. As a result of this economic pressure, the treatment of the slaves improved.

By 1800 the slavery laws which Basil the Wolf had introduced in 1654 had been forgotten, and the treatment of the slaves had become a matter of the whim of those in charge of the estates or the monasteries where they worked. The Ottoman court ratified attempts to make the laws more stringent and in 1818 incorporated new edicts into the Wallachian Penal Code, among them

§2 "Gypsies are born slaves",
§3 "Anyone born of a mother who is a slave, is also a slave",
§5 "Any owner has the right to sell or give away his slaves", and
§6 "Any Gypsy without an owner is the property of the Prince".

The Russians, however, overturned Ottoman rule in 1826, and Paul Kisseleff was appointed to be the governor in 1829. He was a deeply religious man and firmly opposed to slavery but, partly because of pressure

Bills of sale for groups of slaves, dated 1557 and 1558.

from the boyars, he did not abolish it. Instead, in 1833 he incorporated strict, conservative revisions in the Moldavian Civil Code, including the following:

§II (154) "Legal unions cannot take place between free persons and slaves",

§II (162) "Marriage between slaves cannot take place without their owner's consent",

§II (174) "The price of a slave must be fixed by the Tribunal, according to his age, condition and profession", and

§II (176) "If anyone has taken a female slave as a   Goldwashers in Wallachia,
concubine, she will become free after his death. If   eighteenth century.
he has had any children by her, they will also
become free".

By the middle of the nineteenth century, economic and social changes
were beginning to affect the principalities. The more efficient use of farm
machinery introduced by the Industrial Revolution, both in America and
in south-eastern Europe, was making the ownership, care and feeding of
slaves a liability rather than an asset, and movements calling for abolition
in the West, brought into Romania by students returning from the
Sorbonne University in France, were a cause for self-examination.
Moldavia and Wallachia were keen to be regarded as a part of the new,
forward looking Europe, and took France as its model; slavery was being
seen more and more as inhumane, primitive and old fashioned.

Desrrobireja: Abolition

By 1790 *robie* no longer existed in Transylvania, where it was abandoned
over half a century earlier than in Moldavia and Wallachia. This was
probably because that part of Europe had always had stronger links with
the Austro-Hungarian Empire than with Ottoman rule, and therefore was
more directly influenced by western capitalism; it wasn't until the 1830s
that calls for its abolition began to be heard in the principalities to the

De la fii şi moştenitorii
de răposatului
SERDAR NICOLAE NICA
de Bucureşti
sunt

200

de familie de ţigani
de vînzare.

Bărbaţii sunt sclavi excelenţi de curte, adică ţigani de moşie  aurari, cismari, muzicanţi, şi muncitori agricultori. Vînzarea nu osa conţina de mai puţin de cinci sclavi pă rînd. Preţul pe persoană atunci osa fie doua ducate. Osa fie preparaţi ca deobicei şi bazat pe primirea banilor, cumpărătorul. Va fi asigurat de un serviciu adecvat.

Offer of a sale that appeared in 1845 in the Bucharest newspaper *Luna*. It says "From the sons and heirs of Serdar Nicolae Nica of Bucharest, there are 200 Gypsy families for sale. The men are excellent slaves of the court, which is to say estate slaves: gold-washers, cobblers, musicians and field hands. The sale will consist of not fewer than five slaves at a time; the price therefore will be two ducats. They will be made ready in the usual way, and with payment the buyer may be assured of the most attentive service".

south. The smaller landowners who were not able to afford farm machinery and who still relied on their slaves nevertheless continued to oppose abolition vigorously. But here too manufactured goods began to compete with goods produced by the *ţigani* and the price of slaves started to drop catastrophically. Responding to this, in 1837 Governor Alexandru Ghica freed those on the estates under his jurisdiction and allowed them to speak Romani and practice their customs. This only affected a tiny fraction (perhaps one in a thousand) of the overall slave population, but it set the pattern for others to follow: Mihai Sturdza freed his slaves in Moldavia in 1842 and in 1847 the Wallachian church did likewise. On 25 September 1848 students demonstrated publicly in Bucharest, tearing up and burning a copy of the statutes relating to slavery. They also successfully replaced the government with their own provisional party that immediately called for abolition, proclaiming that "The Romanian people reject the inhuman and barbaric practice of owning slaves, and announce the immediate freedom of all Gypsies who belong to individual owners". This freedom was short-lived, however, for less than three months later their interim government was overthrown by the Russian-Turkish Convention that promptly brought back many of the old laws, including those legalizing the ownership of human beings. It is likely that many of the slaves never even knew about their two months of freedom but for those who did, their return to enslavement must have been a terrible blow.

The new government appointed Alexandru Ghica and Barbu Ştirbei to their Council, where they served from 1849 to 1855. In that year, Ghica's cousin Gregory was made Prince of Moldavia, and Ştirbei was appointed Governor of Wallachia. Gregory was a weak man and, while he claimed to deplore slavery, he took no steps to abolish it, making only a token show of sympathy by passing a law that forbade children to be sold separately from their parents. It

The job of torturer (*torturari*) was one of the tasks left to the slaves.

was because of the repeated urgings of his eldest daughter, Natalia Balş and his advisor, Edward Grenier, that he finally brought the matter before the Moldavian General Assembly telling them that:

> For many years, slavery has been abolished in all the civilised states of the Old World; only the principalities of Moldavia and Wallachia retain this humiliating vestige of a barbaric society. It is a social disgrace.

To its great credit the Assembly voted unanimously for abolition and the bill was passed on 23 December 1855. The Wallachian Assembly did the same on 8 February the following year. However, complete legal freedom did not come until 1864, two years after the creation of Romania as a single country, when Prince Ioan Couza restored the Romanies to the estates on which they had formerly worked, this time not as slaves but as free people, and Mihail Kogălniceanu, now leader of the new nation, passed a law that abolished serfdom and redistributed the land to the peasantry. It was also at this time that – in law at least – the word *ţigan* stopped being used as a synonym for 'slave' and instead began to refer to the ethnic population.

One estimate lists the number of slaves at about 600,000 at the time of their emancipation. Writing at this time, J A Vaillant dedicated his

Runaway *Netoţi* being returned to their owner.

book on Romanies to Alexandru and Gregory Ghica with the words:

Those who shed tears of compassion for the Negroes of Africa, of whom the American Republic makes its slaves, should give a kind thought to this short history of the Gypsies of India, of whom the European monarchies make their 'Negroes'. These men, wanderers from Asia, will never again be itinerant; these slaves shall be *free*.

However, following their liberation nothing was done to educate or reorient the freed slaves and bring them into society; instead, it was their former owners who were paid by the government for their loss.

There is very little accessible literature on the period of Balkan slavery (but see Hancock, 1987), though it has been dealt with in fiction by the Romanian authors Bogdan Haşdeu, who wrote an account of the sixteenth century slave Stefan Razvan in his book *Razvan and Vidra*, and Vasile Alecsandri, who wrote a novel about a slave in his *Story of a Gold Coin*. Both of those appeared in the mid-nineteenth century; in the twentieth century two fictionalized accounts of slavery have been published, Roberte Roleine's *Prince of One Summer* (1978) and Matéo Maximoff's *The Price of Liberty* (1955).

The enslavement of Romanies in other places

While we know most about the enslavement of Romanies in the Balkans, our people have been similarly subjugated at different times in other parts of the world as well. This was sometimes simply because of their identity as Romanies, and sometimes because they were categorised

along with anyone else whose social status made
them subject to such treatment. In sixteenth century
England King Edward VI passed a law stating that
Romanies be "branded with a *V* on their breast, and
then enslaved for two years", and if they escaped and
were recaptured, they were then to be branded with an

Romanian students
publicly burn the slavery
statutes, Bucharest,
25 September 1848.

S and made slaves for life. During the same period in Spain, according to
a decree issued in 1538, Romanies were enslaved for their whole lives to
their accusers as a punishment for escaping from prison. Spain had
already begun shipping Romanies to the Americas in the fifteenth century; three were transported by Columbus to the Caribbean on his third
voyage in 1498. Spain's later *solución americana* involved the shipping
of Romani slaves to its colony in eighteenth century Louisiana. An Afro-
Romani community today lives there in St Martin's Parish and reportedly
there is another one in central Cuba, both descended from intermarriage
between the two enslaved peoples. In the sixteenth century, Portugal
shipped Romanies as an unwilling labour force to its colonies in
Maranhão (now part of Brazil), Angola and even India, the Romanies'
country of origin that they had left five centuries earlier. They were made
Slaves of the Crown in eighteenth century Russia during the reign of
Catherine the Great, while in Scotland during the same period they were

Romanies trekking out of
Romania following the
abolition of slavery.

employed 'in a state of slavery' in the coal mines.
England and Scotland had shipped Romanies to
Virginia and the Caribbean as slaves during the seventeenth and eighteenth centuries; one English visitor to
Jamaica in the 1790s described seeing "many Gypsies,
subject from the age of eleven to thirty to the prostitution and lust of
overseers, book-keepers, negroes, and taken into keeping by gentlemen
who paid exorbitant hire for their use". It is likely that the Romani presence in the Caribbean and South America has contributed some elements
to the local cultures, perhaps in music and dress; Moraes (1886:6) wrote
that "the Brazilian nation, from the highest to the lowest, is strongly tinc-
tured with Gypsy blood", while Groome (1899:*xvij*) made a similar
observation about the Romani presence in the West Indies.

Questions

1   What caused slavery to become established?
2   What were the different categories of slaves, and how is that
    reflected today?
3   Who were the *netoţi*?
4   What led to abolition?
5   Were Romanies enslaved in other parts of the world?

CHAPTER THREE

The *Buxljaripe:* Out into Europe

N ot all Romanies were taken into slavery in Wallachia and Moldavia. While it is impossible to determine the exact percentage we might estimate that perhaps half of the population was held in this condition, while the other half was able to continue moving on into the rest of Europe before the slavery laws became rigidly enforced. We know too that throughout the five and a half centuries of slavery, there was a constant trickle of escapees leaving the principalities.

The first Romanies that the Europeans met were very different from any of the local populations – far more distinct than we are today. They were mostly dark-skinned, and wore unfamiliar clothing and spoke a language nobody recognised. They were neither Christian, nor Jewish, nor Muslim, and seemed to have no country of their own. And most of all, they were extremely reluctant to let outsiders – the *gadže* – get too close.

It soon became clear that they were not Turks, and had no interest in spreading Islam throughout Europe, even though many had indeed arrived with the Ottoman troops. The first Romanies went to great lengths to present themselves not only as Christians, but as especially devout Christians on religious pilgrimages, a ploy already being used by numbers of itinerant European groups such as the Rubins, Coquillarts, Convertis and Golliards because it brought them special, if only temporary, privileges. They were not a threat to Christendom, but this was realised much later in northern Europe than it was in southern Europe, where people encountered Turks and could easily compare the two populations; in the northern lands practically nobody knew what Turks looked like, and Romanies in the German-speaking territories and in Scandinavia were thought to be them and were treated with great *top:* A letter of safe conduct for Romanies signed by Pope Martin, AD 1483. *bottom:* A letter of safe conduct for Romanies signed by King Frederick II, AD 1442.

suspicion and hostility. This, together with the other factors mentioned here, helped lay the foundation for the prejudice against Romanies that is so widespread in Europe today and is dealt with in more detail in Chapter 5.

What the Europeans thought

There was already an 'outsider' population in Europe when the first Romanies arrived – the Jews. Even before the Romanies, the Jews were confronted with suspicion and hostility from the Europeans, and for the same reasons: they were not Christians, they had no country of their own and they preferred to keep to themselves. It didn't take much effort on the part of the European peasantry to imagine a link between both our peoples, especially since each had a perceived connection with Egypt. It was believed by some that Romanies were the Jews who had fled from Pharaoh Ramses II, or even perhaps the Egyptians who had chased them; it was thought by others that Romanies were descendants of Jews who had remained hidden for years in caves following mediaeval pogroms against them, and who had now re-emerged; still others believed that we were the offspring of Jews and Christian vagabonds. The notion of a Jewish origin has not been completely abandoned; one website by Im Nin'alu (at *http://web.tiscali.it/imninalu/english.htm*) is devoted to making this case in great detail. One writer said that we came from the interbreeding of Egyptians, Ethiopians and troglodytes (cave dwellers). It was said that our ancestors were Phoenicians, or else Babylonians. The Bible also provided some possible origins: as metalworkers, the first Romanies were identified with Cain (Genesis 4:15) and believed to be cursed never to settle; as tent-dwellers, they were identified as being descendants of Rechab and Jonadab (Jeremiah, 35:5–10). A common belief, and one still prevalent, is that we weren't really a separate ethnic population at all, but a mix of people made up of the criminal fringes of many different European societies, "red-ochred rascals" as one observer called us, who deliberately darkened our faces with clay or the juice of walnuts or berries:

> These gipsies are nothing else than a congregated troop of bad characters, [who …] stain their faces with green nutshells in order to increase their ugliness and that they may more easily induce the inexperienced to believe that they come from the hot oriental countries (de Peyster, 1887:15).

In 1633, Philip IV of Spain declared that we didn't even exist, that we were really only Spanish people who had made up an artificial language. Just as Empress Maria Theresa ordered 150 years later in Hungary, Philip made it illegal to speak our language or call ourselves Romanies. These explanations, though all quite wrong, at least acknowledged that we were human. There was a belief at one time that we had come from the Moon!

The Romani language too has been accounted for in a number of inventive ways. It was commonly thought to be a made-up 'secret' jargon, used specifically for the purpose of discussing criminal activity: "They form for themselves a peculiar language and separate dialect in order thus to appear more foreign and that they may communicate with each other concerning their plans without being understood by other people" (de Peyster, op cit., 15). The early nineteenth century writer Johann Gustav Büsching claimed that "the Gypsy language is a mixture of corrupt words from Wallachian, Slavic and Hungarian and other nations", while another wrote that it was a mixture of German, Hebrew and nonsense words. Yet another thought that Romani was Nubian, from Africa. One man addressed some Romanies in 'Egyptian', presumably Coptic or Arabic, which wasn't understood, and expressed surprise when the reply came in Greek.

It is difficult to understand why the Europeans' reaction to our people was as intense as it was. Within a short space of time, laws began to be created in different countries to regulate the movement and treatment of Romanies, and by 1417 the first anti-Romani law was issued in Germany with forty-eight more being issued in that country over the following three centuries. In 1568 Pope Pius V banished Romanies from the realm of the Holy Roman Church, and in 1721 Emperor Karl VI called for the extermination of Romanies everywhere throughout his domain. All those crossing into Bohemia in 1740 were ordered to be killed, and in 1782 some 200 were tortured and executed following false charges of cannibalism. In Spain, Hungary and colonial Brazil it was illegal to call oneself a Romani or to speak our language; in places such as England and Finland, it was illegal even to be *born* a Romani – in other words, our ancestors were breaking the law simply by existing. It would be easy to fill a book with accounts of such mistreatment from every country in Europe. While these are shocking and seemingly endless, and certainly should not be forgotten, it is of more contemporary relevance to understand why the phenomenon of antigypsyism exists, and what can be done about it; we are, after all, a people who have never started a war, who have never tried to take over a foreign government and who have never been an economic or political threat to anyone. In fact, if anything typifies us as a people, it is our desire to keep to ourselves.

In Eastern Europe especially, four decades of communism instilled a perspective into educational systems that placed little emphasis on history. And yet the present-day situation of the Romani population in Europe can *only* be properly understood if it is seen in its historical context, as the end of a continuum stretching back across the centuries. While it is easy to look at the sad condition of Romanies today, at the ghettos, the begging, the high unemployment and crime rates and to react negatively, two questions must be asked: first – what series of events, since the Romanies first arrived in Europe, have brought the present-day population to this miserable state, and second, do Romanies live this way as a matter of choice? Given a more attractive option, would they take it?

There are many who really believe that we enjoy squalour; an anonymous writer for a Victorian magazine wrote that Romanies live "… in the greatest misery and filth, in fact the dirtier their huts, the better they like them" (*Anon.*, 1856:274). Some find this amusing – there are even unkind cartoons based on this very wrong assumption (pp. 98 and 99). There are those who believe that we want only to take, and give nothing back, and that we have contributed nothing at all to 'civilisation'. And there are those who think that we believe that we have a right to steal from and cheat the *gadže*. Of course, there is no denying what is there plainly to see. But it has to be understood, and addressed in the right way, if things are to improve. This means a change not only in the situation of Romanies but also in the attitudes of many people towards us. When Vaclav Havel said that a country's treatment of its Romani population would stand as the litmus test for tolerance throughout Europe generally he knew that everyone, both Romani and non-Romani, would either suffer or prosper from the outcome.

Questions

1 What first impressions did the Europeans have of the Romanies? Who did they think they were?
2 Why were Romanies marginalized after arriving in Europe?
3 Do you think that the Romanies also marginalized the non-Romani people? Why?

CHAPTER FOUR

O Baro Porrajmos – The Holocaust

The motives invoked to justify the death of the Gypsies were the same as
those ordering the murder of the Jews, and the methods employed for the one
were identical with those employed for the other

(Novitch, Ghetto Fighters' House, Israel, 1968:3).

The greatest tragedy to befall the European Romani population was
the attempt to eradicate it as part of the Nazis' plan to have a
'Gypsy-free' Europe. Although it wasn't the first governmental plan to
exterminate Romanies (German Emperor Karl VI had previously issued
such an order in 1721), it was by far the most devastating, ultimately
destroying over half of the Romani population in Nazi-occupied Europe.
Romanies were the only other population besides the Jews who were targeted for extermination on racial/ethnic grounds in the Final Solution.
Note that in Germany, the traditional Romani population calls itself Sinti,
while the word *Zigeuner* is the German equivalent of 'Gypsy' and should
be avoided. In Romani, the Holocaust is referred to as the *Baro Porrajmos*, or 'great devouring' of human life. *Porrajmos* is an ugly word, well
chosen for the ugliest event in our history. It can also mean 'rape', as
well as 'gaping' as in shock or horror. Some people hesitate to say the
word out loud.

When the Nazis came to power in 1933, German laws against Romanies
had already been in effect for hundreds of years. The persecution of the
Romani people began almost as soon as they first arrived in German-
speaking lands because as outsiders, they were, without knowing it,
breaking the Hanseatic laws which made it a punishable offence not to
have a permanent home or job, and not to be on the taxpayers' register.

They were also accused of being spies for the Muslims, whom few Germans had ever met, but about whom they had heard many frightening stories; it was not illegal to murder a Romani and there were sometimes 'Gypsy hunts' in which Romanies were tracked down and killed like wild animals; forests were set on fire to drive out any Romanies who might have been hiding there.

By the nineteenth century, scholars in Germany and elsewhere in Europe were writing about Romanies and Jews as being inferior beings and "the excrement of humanity"; even Darwin, writing in 1871, singled out our two populations as not being "culturally advanced" like other "territorially settled" peoples. This crystallized into specifically racist attitudes in the writing of Knox, Tetzner, Gobineau and others. By the 1880s, Chancellor von Bismarck reinforced some of the discriminatory laws, stating that Romanies were to be dealt with "especially severely" if apprehended.

In or shortly after 1890, a conference on 'The Gypsy Scum' (*Das Zigeunergeschmeiß*) was held in Swabia, at which the military was given full authority to keep Romanies on the move. In 1899 the Englishman Houston Chamberlain, who was the composer Richard Wagner's son-in-law, wrote a book called *The Foundations of the Nineteenth Century*, in which he argued for the building of a "newly shaped … and … especially deserving Aryan race". It was used to justify the promotion of ideas about German racial superiority and for any oppressive action taken against members of 'inferior' populations. In that same year, the 'Gypsy Information Agency' was set up in Munich under the direction of Alfred Dillmann, which began cataloguing data on all Romanies throughout the German lands. The results of this were published in 1905 in Dillmann's *Zigeuner-Buch*, which laid the foundations for what was to happen to our people in the Holocaust thirty-five years later.

The *Zigeuner-Buch* is nearly 350 pages long, and consists of three parts: first, an introduction stating that Romanies were a "plague" and a "menace" against which the German population had to defend itself

Zigeuner=Buch

herausgegeben zum amtlichen Gebrauche im Auf=
trage des K. B. Staatsminifteriums des Innern vom
Sicherheitsbureau der K. Polizeidirektion München.

⁊

Bearbeitet von

Alfred Dillmann,

Oberregierungsrat bei der K. Polizeidirektion.

⁊

Zu beziehen vom Taxamt der K. Polizeidirektion München.
Preis (ohne Porto) 1 Mark.

⁊

München 1905.
Dr. Wild'fche Buchdruckerei (Gebr. Parcus).

using "ruthless punishments", and which warned of the dangers of mixing the Romani and German gene pools. The second part was a register of all known Romanies, giving genealogical details and criminal record if any, and the third part was a collection of photographs of those same people. Dillmann's ideas about 'race mixing' later became a central part of the Nuremberg Law in Nazi Germany.

Euthanasia was a topical issue in the early twentieth century, and received popular support from such notables as the author H G Wells. In 1920 two Germans, a psychiatrist, Karl Binding and a magistrate, Alfred Hoche, wrote a book called *The Eradication of Lives Undeserving of Life*, a phrase first coined over half a century earlier by Richard Liebich with specific reference to Romanies in 1863 and in 1869 by Kulemann, again referring only to Romanies. Among the three groups that they considered to be "unworthy of life" were the "incurably mentally ill", and it was with this group that Romanies were identified.

Perceived Romani 'criminality' was seen as a transmitted genetic disease, though no account was taken of the centuries of exclusion of the Romanies from German society, which made subsistence theft a necessity for survival (see Chapter 11). A law incorporating the phrase *lives undeserving of life* was put into effect just four months after Hitler became Chancellor of the Third Reich.

During the 1920s, the legal oppression of Romanies in Germany intensified, despite the official statutes of the Weimar Republic that said that all its citizens were equal. In 1920 they were forbidden to enter parks and public baths; in 1925 a conference on 'The Gypsy Question' was held which resulted in the creation of laws requiring unemployed Romanies to be sent to work camps "for reasons of public security", and for all Romanies to be registered with the police. After 1927 everyone, even Romani children, had to carry identification cards bearing their fingerprints and photographs. In 1929, The Central Office for the Fight Against the Gypsies in Germany was established in Munich, and in 1933, just ten days before the Nazis came to power, government officials in Burgenland, Austria, called for the withdrawal of all civil rights from the Romani people.

In September 1935, Romanies became subject to the restrictions of the Nuremberg Law for the Protection of German Blood and Honour, which forbade intermarriage between Germans and 'non-Aryans', specifically Jews, Romanies and people of African descent. In 1937, the National Citizenship Law relegated Romanies and Jews to the status of second-class citizens, depriving them of their civil rights. In the same year, Heinrich Himmler issued a decree entitled "The Struggle Against the Gypsy Plague" which reiterated that Romanies of mixed blood were the most likely to engage in criminal activity, and which required that all information on Romanies be sent from the regional police departments to the Reich Central Office. In their book published in 1943, the Danish sociologists Erik Bartels and Gudrun Brun echoed this position, evidently unaware that the sterilization of Romanies had already been in effect for a decade:

> The pure gypsies present no great problem, if only we realise that their mentality does not allow of their admittance to the well-ordered general society ... the mixed gypsies cause considerably greater difficulties

Der Reichsführer-**ϟϟ**
und
Chef der Deutschen Polizei
im Reichsministerium des Innern

S-Kr.1 Nr.557/38.

Berlin SW 11, den 24. März 193.
Prinz-Albrecht-Straße 8

An das

   Staatsministerium des Innern

   in M ü n c h e n .

18

Betrifft: Zigeunerfrage.

- - - - -

                  Als Anlage übersende ich mit der Bitte
      um Stellungnahme einen ersten Vorentwurf, der
      als Grundlage für die weitere Behandlung der
      Zigeunerfrage dienen soll. Gegenüber den bis-
      herigen Länderbestimmungen enthält dieser
      vorläufige Entwurf vor allem den Gedanken,
      die endgültige Lösung der Zigeunerfrage nach
      rassischen Gesichtspunkten einzuleiten. In die-
      ser Hinsicht ist außer der Vorbereitung der
      Erfassung aller Zigeuner vor allem der Hin-
      weis auf Absatz A II 1 e des Runderlasses vom
      14.Dezember 1937 - Pol.S-Kr.3 Nr.1682/37-2098 -
      betreffend vorbeugende Verbrechensbekämpfung
      durch die Polizei (nicht veröffentlicht) von
      Bedeutung, nach dem insbesondere die asozialen
      Mischlinge in polizeiliche Vorbeugungshaft ge-
      nommen werden können.

                                                     Der

The first mention in print of the *endgültige Lösung der Zigeunerfrage*, 24 March 1938.

(… nothing good has) come from a crossing between a gipsy and a white person … Germany is at present contemplating the introduction of provisions of sterilization is the case of such families (1943:5).

Calling a population vermin, or a disease, rather than

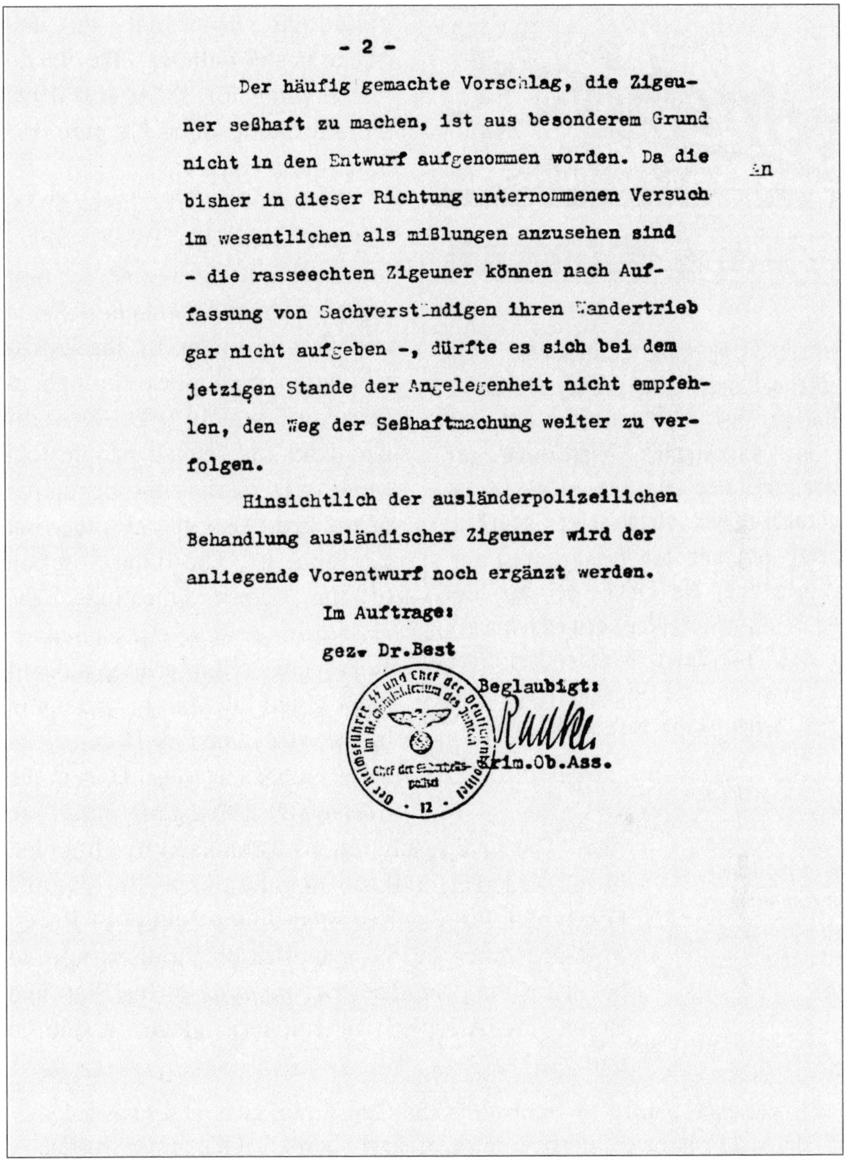

- 2 -

Der häufig gemachte Vorschlag, die Zigeuner seßhaft zu machen, ist aus besonderem Grund
nicht in den Entwurf aufgenommen worden. Da die   An
bisher in dieser Richtung unternommenen Versuch
im wesentlichen als mißlungen anzusehen sind
- die rasseechten Zigeuner können nach Auf-
fassung von Sachverständigen ihren Wandertrieb
gar nicht aufgeben -, dürfte es sich bei dem
jetzigen Stande der Angelegenheit nicht empfeh-
len, den Weg der Seßhaftmachung weiter zu ver-
folgen.

Hinsichtlich der ausländerpolizeilichen
Behandlung ausländischer Zigeuner wird der
anliegende Vorentwurf noch ergänzt werden.

Im Auftrage:

gez. Dr.Best

Beglaubigt:

Runke

Krim.Ob.Ass.

recognising it as being part of the human family is a technique used to
dehumanize it and to distance it from society. Such terms were constantly used to refer to Jews and Romanies in the Third Reich in an effort
to desensitize the general population to the increasingly harsh treatment
being meted out against them; after all, vermin and diseases need to be

Preis 18 Pfennig   München, 21. Februar 1939
                                                    1. Jahrgang · Nummer 4

ns.-Rechtsspiegel

Kampfblatt für deutsches

Organ des Reichsrechtsamtes der NSDAP.

In seinem Erlaß vom 8. Dezember 1938
hat der Reichsführer ½ und Chef der Deutschen Polizei im Reichsministerium des
Innern die allgemeinen Richtlinien zur
umfassenden Bekämpfung der Zigeuner im
ganzen großdeutschen Reichsgebiet gegeben.

Der Erlaß geht von den Erfahrungen und
Erkenntnissen aus, die bisher bei der Bekämpfung der Zigeunerplage gewonnen wur-
den. Er will, und damit packt er das Übel
an der Wurzel an, die Zigeunerfrage aus
dem Wesen dieser Rasse heraus lösen.

Notice in the 21 February
1939 issue of the Nazi
paper *Rechtsspiegel*
announcing Himmler's
decree of the previous
8 December.

eradicated. Disturbingly, this language is still with us – the *Badische Zeitung* for 28 August 1992 carried the headline "A pure disease, these Gypsies!"

Between 13–18 June 1938, 'Gypsy Clean-Up Week' (*Zigeuneraufräumungswoche*, also called *Aktion Arbeitschau Reich* and *Bettlerwoche* in the documentation) took place throughout Germany which, like Kristallnacht for the Jewish people that same year, marked the beginning of the end. Also in 1938, the first reference to "The Final Solution of the Gypsy Question" (*die endgültige Lösung der Zigeunerfrage*) appeared in print in a document dated 24 March, and again in an order issued by Himmler on 8 December that year. Thus in the *Auschwitz Memorial Book* we find "The final resolution, as formulated by Himmler, in his 'Decree for Basic Regulations to Resolve the Gypsy Question as Required by the Nature of Race', of 8 December, 1938, meant that preparations were to begin for the *complete extermination* of the Sinti and Roma" (SMAB,1993:*xiv*, emphasis added). It said, in part,

Experience gained in combatting the Gypsy nuisance, and knowledge derived from race-biological research, have shown that the proper method of attacking the Gypsy problem seems to be to treat it as a matter of race. Experience shows that part-Gypsies play the greatest role in Gypsy criminality … It has therefore become necessary to establish the racial affinity of every Gypsy living in Germany and of every vagrant living a Gypsy-like existence. I therefore decree that all settled and non-settled Gypsies, and also all vagrants living a Gypsy-like existence, are to be registered

with the Central Office for Combatting the Gypsy Nuisance … the aim of measures taken by the State to defend the homogeneity of the German nation must be the physical separation of Gypsydom from the German nation.

Romani prisoners in the concentration camp at Bergen-Belsen.

This was announced to the general public in the *NS-Rechtspiegel* on the 21 February 1939. In 1938 Himmler also issued his criteria for biological and racial evaluation which determined that each Romani's family background was to be investigated going back for three generations; the Nazis' racial motive for exterminating Romanies is clear from the fact that they even targeted Romani-*like* people, taking no chances lest the German population be contaminated with undetected Romani blood. Kenrick (1998:74-5) writes:

> In general, a person with one Jewish grandparent was not affected in the Nazi anti-Jewish legislation, whereas one-eighth 'gypsy blood' was considered strong enough to outweigh seven-eighths of German blood – so dangerous were the Gypsies considered.

This was twice as strict as the criteria determining who was Jewish; had

Robert Ritter photographing Sinti Romanies.

the same standard applied to Romanies, nearly 20,000 would have escaped death. On 16 December 1941 Himmler issued the order to have Romanies throughout western Europe deported to Auschwitz-Birkenau for extermination.

In 1939 Johannes Behrendt of the Office of Racial Hygiene issued a brief stating that "[a]ll Gypsies should be treated as hereditarily sick; the only solution is elimination. The aim should therefore be the elimination without hesitation of this defective element in the population". In January 1940 the first mass genocidal action of the Holocaust took place when 250 Romani children from Brno were murdered in Buchenwald, where they were used as guinea-pigs to test the efficacy of the Zyklon-B cyanide gas crystals that were later used in the gas chambers (Proester, 1940). In June 1940 Hitler ordered the extermination of all Jews, Romanies and communist political functionaries in the entire Soviet Union. Reinhard Heydrich, who was Head of the Reich Main Security Office and the leading organisational architect of the Nazi Final Solution, ordered the Einsaztkommandos to kill all Jews, Romanies and mental

patients, although not all of the documentation
regarding its complete details, for either Jews or
Romanies, has been found. Müller-Hill (1988:58-9)
writes:

Robert Ritter collecting data
on a Sinti woman

> Heydrich, who had been entrusted with the 'final solution of the Jewish
> question' on 31st July 1941, shortly after the German invasion of the
> USSR, also included the Gypsies in his 'final solution'... The senior SS
> officer and Chief of Police for the East, Dr. Landgraf, in Riga, informed
> Rosenberg's Reich Commissioner for the East, Lohse, of the inclusion of
> the Gypsies in the 'final solution'. Thereupon, Lohse gave the order, on
> 24th December 1941, that the Gypsies should be given the same treatment
> as the Jews.

Burleigh and Wippermann (1991:121-25) write further that:

> A conference on racial policy organised by Heydrich took place in Berlin
> on 21st September 1939, which may have decided upon a 'Final Solution'
> of the 'Gypsy Question'. According to the scant minutes which have
> survived, four issues were decided: the concentration of Jews in towns;
> their relocation to Poland; the removal of 30,000 Gypsies to Poland, and
> the systematic deportation of Jews to German incorporated territories
> using goods trains. An express letter sent by the Reich Main Security

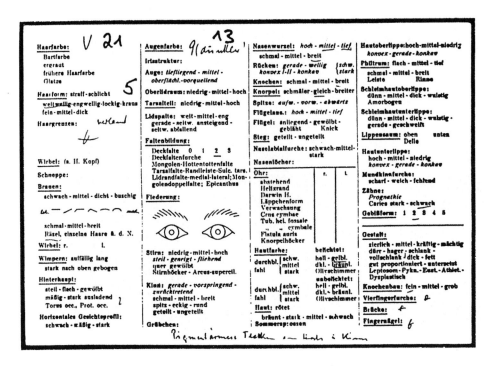

One of Ritter's forms for recording biological data on Romani prisoners.

Office on 17th October 1939 to its local agents mentioned that the 'Gypsy Question will shortly be regulated throughout the territory of the Reich'. ... At about this time, Adolf Eichmann made the recommendation that the 'Gypsy Question' be solved simultaneously with the 'Jewish Question' ... Himmler signed the order dispatching Germany's Sinti and Roma to Auschwitz on 16th December 1942. The 'Final Solution' of the 'Gypsy Question' had begun.

Himmler's order stated that "all Gypsies are to be deported to the Zigeunerlager at Auschwitz concentration camp, with no regard to their degree of racial impurity". The *Memorial Book* for the Romanies who died at Auschwitz-Birkenau also says (SMAB, 1993:3):

The Himmler decree of December 16th 1942 (Auschwitz-Erlaß), according to which the Gypsies should be deported to Auschwitz-Birkenau, had the same meaning for the Gypsies that the conference at Wannsee on January 20th 1942, had for the Jews. This decree, and the bulletin that followed on January 29th 1943, can thus be regarded as a logical consequence of the decision taken at Wannsee. After it had been decided that the fate of the Jews was to end in mass extermination, it was natural for the other

group of racially persecuted people, the Gypsies, to become victims of the same policy, which finally even included soldiers in the Wehrmacht.

Eva Justin, here collecting data for Robert Ritter, was called *Loli Tschai* (the "red girl") by the Romani inmates because of her red hair.

In a paper delivered in Washington in 1987, at a conference on the fate of the non-Jewish victims of the Holocaust sponsored by the US Holocaust Memorial Council, Dr Erika Thurner of the Institut für Neuere Geschichte und Zeitgeschichte at the University of Linz stated that:

> Heinrich Himmler's infamous Auschwitz decree of December 16th, 1942, can be seen as the final stage of the final solution of the Gypsy Question. The decree served as the basis for complete extermination. According to the implementation instructions of 1943, all Gypsies, irrespective of their racial mix, were to be assigned to concentration camps. The concentration camp for Gypsy families at Auschwitz-Birkenau was foreseen as their final destination... opposed to the fact that the decision to seek a final solution for the Gypsy Question came at a later date than that of the Jewish Question, the first steps taken to exterminate the Gypsies were initiated prior to this policy decision.

This order appears to have been the result of a direct decision from Hitler

Lebensschicksale
artfremd erzogener Zigeunerkinder
und ihrer Nachkommen

Inaugural-Dissertation

zur

Erlangung des Doktorgrades

genehmigt von der

Mathematisch-Naturwissenschaftlichen Fakultät

der Friedrich-Wilhelms-Universität
zu Berlin

von

Eva Justin
aus Dresden

Tag der Promotion: 5. November 1943
Tag der mündlichen Prüfung: 24. März 1943

Eva Justin produced a dissertation based on her work with Ritter; it attempted to demonstrate the inherited mental deficiency of school age Romani children.

himself (Milton, 1992:10). Breitman (1991:164) reproduced the statement issued by Security Police Commander Bruno Streckenbach following a policy meeting with Hitler and Heydrich held in Pretsch in June, 1940, *viz.* that "[t]he Führer has ordered the liquidation of all Jews, Gypsies and communist political functionaries in the entire area of the Soviet Union". SS Officer Percy Broad, who worked in the political division at Auschwitz and who participated directly in the murders of several thousand prisoners there, recollected in a memoir twenty-five years later that "… it was the will of the all-powerful Reichsführer to have the Gypsies disappear from the face of the earth" (1966:41). On 4 August 1944, some 2,900 Romanies were gassed and cremated in a single action at Auschwitz-Birkenau, during what is remembered as *Zigeunernacht.*

Determining the percentage or number of Romanies who died in the Holocaust has not been easy. Bernard Streck (in Rakelmann, 1979) noted that "any attempts to express Romani casualties in terms of numbers … cannot be verified by means of lists or card-indexes or camp files; most of the Gypsies died in eastern or southern Europe, shot by execution troops or fascist gang members". Much of the Nazi documentation still remains to be analysed and, as Streck intimates, many murders were not recorded since they took place in the fields and forests where Romanies were arrested. There are no accurate figures either for the pre-war Romani population in Europe, though the Nazi Party's official census of 1939 estimated it to be about two million, certainly an under-representation. Regarding numbers, König (1989:87-9) says:

> The count of half a million Sinti and Roma murdered between 1939 and 1945 is too low to be tenable; for example in the Soviet Union many of the Romani dead were listed under non-specific labels such as *Liquidierungsübrigen* [remainder to be liquidated], 'hangers-on' and 'partisans'...The final number of the dead Sinti and Roma may never be determined. We do not know precisely how many were brought into the concentration camps; not every concentration camp produced statistical material; moreover, Sinti and Roma are often listed under the heading of remainder to be liquidated, and do not appear in the statistics for Gypsies.

Sophie Ehrhart was a principal member of Ritter's staff.

In the eastern territories, in Russia especially, Romani deaths were sometimes counted into the records under the heading of Jewish deaths. The *Memorial Book* (SMAB, 1993:2) also discusses the means of killing Romanies:

> Unlike the Jews, the overwhelming majority of whom were murdered in the gas chambers at Birkenau, Belzec, Treblinka and all the other mass extermination camps, the Gypsies outside the Reich were massacred at many places, sometimes only a few at a time, and sometimes by the hundreds. In the *Generalgouvernement* [the eastern territories] alone, 150 sites of Gypsy massacres are known. Research on the Jewish Holocaust can rely on comparison of pre- and post-war census data to help determine the numbers of victims in the countries concerned. However, this is not possible for the Gypsies, as it was only rarely that they were included in national census data. Therefore it is an impossible task to find the actual

This two-year-old boy, Schutka Weinrich, was a special pet of Joseph Mengele, who carried him everywhere. He made him dance and sing, but casually tossed him into the oven when he decided that he'd grown tired of him.

number of Gypsy victims in Poland, Yugoslavia, White Ruthenia and the Ukraine, the lands that probably had the greatest numbers of victims.

In 1995 the late Dr Sybil Milton, then senior historian at the US Holocaust Memorial Research Institute in Washington, said "[w]e believe that something between a half-million and a million-and-a-half Roma and Sinti were murdered in Nazi Germany and occupied Europe between 1939 and 1945" (Latham, 1995:2). Significantly, the same figure appeared again in a November 2001 report issued by the International Organization for Migration (the *IOM*), a body designated to locate and compensate surviving Romani Holocaust victims. The brief states that "[r]ecent research indicates that up to 1.5 million Roma perished during the Nazi era" (Heine, 2001:1). It is certainly a fact that interviews by trained Romani-speaking personnel who have obtained testimonials at first-hand from claimants throughout central and eastern Europe have already shed startling new light on this issue: the number of Romani survivors is far in excess of anything previously estimated. By extrapolation, and from the same eyewitness accounts documented in recent years, the numbers of Romanies who perished at the hands of the Nazis has also been grossly underestimated. Eventually, these revised figures will find their way into the public record.

Since the end of the Second World War, Germany's response regarding the Romani people has been less than exemplary. Nobody was called to testify on behalf of the Romani victims at the Nuremberg Trials, and no war crimes reparations have ever been paid to Romanies as a people. Today, neo-Nazi activity in many parts of central and Eastern Europe makes the Romanies its prime target of racial violence. Kenrick (1998:4) summarized the situation after 1945 very well:

Hyg.-bakt. Unters.-Stelle
der Waffen-SS, Südost

29. JUN. 1944

Auschwitz OS., am **29.Juni 1944.**

Anliegend wird übersandt:

(12-jähriges Kind)

Material: **Kopf einer Leiche** entnommen am

zu untersuchen auf **Histologische Schnitte**

Name, Vorname:

Dienstgrad, Einheit: **siehe Anlage**

Klinische Diagnose:

Anschrift der einsendenden Dienststelle: **H.-Krankenbau**
Zigeunerlager Auschwitz II, B II e

Bemerkungen:

Der 1.Lagerarzt

K.L.Auschwitz II

SS-Hauptsturmführer.
(Stempel, Unterschrift)

In the first years following the end of the Nazi domination of Europe, the Gypsy community was in disarray. The small [Romani] educational and cultural organisations that had existed before 1939 had been destroyed. The family structure was broken with the death of the older people – the guardians of the traditions. While in the camps, the Gypsies had been unable to keep up their customs – the Romanía – concerning the preparation of food and the washing of clothes. They solved the psychological problems by not speaking about the time in the camps. Only a small number of Gypsies could read or write, so they could not tell their own story. But also they were unwilling to tell their own stories to others, and few others were interested anyway. In the many books written describing the Nazi period and the persecution of the Jews, Gypsies usually appear as a footnote or small section.

Medical documents requesting the head of a Romani child for experimentation, dated 29 June 1944 and signed by Joseph Mengele.

We are still a long way from fully understanding the *Porrajmos* and achieving its proper acknowledgment in the classroom; including a section on the *Porrajmos* must be viewed as essential to any Romani Studies curriculum.

An argument which is sometimes made is that the Romanies simply didn't preoccupy the Nazis; we have been called an "afterthought" in Nazi policy, and it has even been said that "the whole Gypsy problem

Back to square one: In 1984 American Romanies demonstrated in Washington to protest the exclusion of our representation on the US Holocaust Memorial Council. President Reagan made our first appointment in 1987, but in 2002 it was taken away by the Bush administration. Once again Romanies have been denied recognition of their history in the Holocaust.

was for Himmler and most other Nazis only a minor irritant" (Bauer, 1994:446). This is neither fair nor true, but can probably be accounted for by the fact that our people were far fewer in number, were much more easily identified and disposed of, and had already been the target of discriminatory policy even before Hitler came to power. It required no massive effort on the part of the Nazis to locate and destroy a population which had no one to take its part. Haberer (2001:212) adds to this:

[Regarding] the persecution of Gypsies, it should be noted that their plight equaled that of the Jews. Their liquidation was part and parcel of the Nazis' agenda to eradicate 'worthless life'. Wrapped up in the Holocaust *per se*, the genocide of the Roma in the East is still very much an untold story. In some ways, their victimization was practiced even more ruthlessly because they held no 'economic value' and were traditionally considered a particular asocial and criminally inclined people [and] more alien in appearance, culture and language.

The United Nations too, did nothing to assist Romanies during or following the Holocaust nor, sadly, were Romanies mentioned anywhere in the documentation of the US War Refugee Board. This is all the more puzzling since the situation was known to the War Crimes Tribunal in Washington as early as 1946, as is evident from file No. 682-PS (USGPO, 1946:496) which contains the text of the meeting between Justice Minister Otto Thierack and Josef Goebbels on 14 September 1942. This stated plainly that

> With regard to the destruction of asocial life, Dr Goebbels is of the opinion that the following groups should be exterminated: *Jews and Gypsies unconditionally*, Poles who have served 3–4 years of penal servitude, and Czechs and Germans who are sentenced to death ... The idea of exterminating them by labour is best (emphasis added).

Nevertheless, the situation is gradually improving. In Germany itself, the handbook and CD-ROM on Holocaust education prepared for teachers and issued by the Press and Information Office of the Federal Government in 2000 makes clear that

The monument to the Romani victims of the *Porrajmos* in the Museumplein in Amsterdam.

> recent historical research in the United States and Germany does not support the conventional argument that the Jews were the only victims of Nazi genocide. True, the murder of Jews by the Nazis differed from the Nazis' killing of political prisoners and foreign opponents because it was based on the genetic origin of the victims and not on their behaviour. The Nazi regime applied a consistent and inclusive policy of extermination based on heredity only against three groups of human beings: the handicapped, Jews, and Sinti and Roma ("Gypsies"). The Nazis killed multitudes, including political and religious opponents, members of the resistance, elites of conquered nations, and homosexuals, but always based these murders on the belief, actions and status of those victims. Different criteria applied only to the murder of the handicapped, Jews, and "Gypsies". Members of these groups could not escape their fate by changing their behavior or belief. They were selected because they existed (Heye et al., 2000:14).

Questions

1 What does *Porrajmos* mean? Why are people upset by this particular word?

2 Could the Nazis' policies directed at 'non-Aryans' be regarded as a kind of 'ethnic cleansing'?

3 Explain what led over time to the Nazis' policy to destroy the European Romani population.

4 Why does there seem to be a reluctance to acknowledging the Nazis' genocidal policy regarding Romanies?

5 Why did they consider "The Final Solution of the Gypsy Question" to be necessary?

6 What has happened to the Romanies who survived the Holocaust in the years since 1945?

7 Do you think that the lack of acknowledgment of the Romanies' plight after the Second World War has any bearing upon their present-day situation?

8 Why is it difficult to estimate the number of Romanies who perished in the *Porrajmos*?

CHAPTER FIVE

Explaining antigypsyism

Roma remain to date the most persecuted people of Europe. Almost
everywhere, their fundamental human rights are threatened. Racist violence
targeting Roma is widespread in the last years. Discrimination against Roma
in employment, education, health care, administrative and other services
is observed in most societies, and hate speech deepens the anti-Romani
stereotypes typical of European public opinion

(ERRC, 2001:5).

In September, 2001, the Council of Europe "issued a blistering con-
demnation of Europe's treatment of the Roma Gypsy community,
saying they are subject to racism, discrimination and violence ... the UN
says they pose Europe's most serious human rights problem" (BBC,
2001). The most powerful recent account of this situation and one that
must be read in order fully to understand the extent of it, is the European
Roma Rights Center's report entitled *Racial Discrimination and Violence
Against Roma in Europe* (Szente, 2001).

Antigypsyism is the treatment of Romanies as less than equals, and
seeking to deny them the same freedoms in society that one wishes for
oneself. This can be institutionalized, that is to say supported by law, or it
can be personal.

Institutionalized antigypsyism in Europe began in the fourteenth century with slavery and continues to this day. The first laws curtailing the
movements of Romanies date from 1416 and the same kind of legislation
may still be found in effect in some places even today; there is still at
least one law against Romanies in the United States.

Institutionalized antigypsyism might not always have the force of law
to support it but may be policy nevertheless: an immigration officer's

"No Gypsies" sign outside a pub in Kent, England, 1966.

decision to refuse entry to a Romani family while letting a non-Romani family in, for example, or a police officer's apprehending and questioning a citizen simply because he is Romani. Employment agencies or airlines which indicate a Romani client's ethnicity on their own paperwork in order to ensure his unequal treatment – both of these situations have been reported since January, 2001 – are examples of this kind of discrimination. They also qualify as institutionalized antigypsyism because they originate within institutionalized society, and those who perpetrate it use their official authority as a weapon. It is personal too, since the decision to discriminate rests with those same individuals.

Personal antigypsyism is far more common. It shows itself daily in a look, or a comment, in a shopkeeper's refusal to serve Romani customers, in an employer's refusal to give a Romani person a job, in a teacher's ignoring a Romani child in class. It shows itself in jokes and cartoons, and it shows itself in acts of physical violence. Where does this discrimination against Romanies come from? It is the result of a combination of historical factors, some of which have been addressed already in this book, which have come together over hundreds of years. These are:

Romanies as foreign intruders and non-Christians

The first Romanies in Europe were associated with the encroachment of the Asiatic invaders and with Islam and were seen as an enemy from the very beginning. Their mistaken identity is reflected in some of the names still applied to Romani populations today, such as Saracens, Tatars, Gypsies, Turks, heathens, etc. Romanies, who entered Europe following the Crusades to reconquer the holy lands in the Middle East were regarded as being a part of the spread of Islam into the West and were persecuted as a result. The Ottoman Turks not only posed a threat to the Christian establishment and blocked access to the Holy Land, but also sealed off routes to the East, thereby affecting trade and the Euro-

"Gypsies not allowed", a sign at a campground near Tilton, New Hampshire (USA).

pean economy. The attitude of the Church also played a major role in creating and perpetuating antigypsyism over the centuries. Ironically, the prejudice which kept Romanies from staying in an area, and which led to their constantly being moved on, created a new suspicion, especially in mediaeval Germany: that they were spies for the Turks. The charge of being enemy spies was also made by the Nazis, and more recently plans to build a site for Romanies next to a Ministry of Defence installation in Surrey in the south of England were abandoned because "it could pose a risk to the security" of the establishment and "allow terrorists near the top-secret site for reconnaissance work" (*Anon.*, 1990). During the Kosovo conflict both Albanians and Serbs expressed fears that the Romani population might be be spying for the other side.

Traditional European societies place tremendous emphasis on the concept of a homeland and national territory, and bitter and bloody wars have been fought to defend them. Terms of address such as *Landsman* or *paisano* or *zemljak* make specific reference to a shared country. A home means stability and permanence; it means being part of a community, where your neighbors recognise you and know exactly where you fit into their social structure. Outsiders meet none of these criteria and, being an unknown quantity, pose a potential threat. At best a people without a country must forever be guests in another's homeland, and at worst unwelcome intruders. In more modern times, people without a country receive less attention and lack an international arena in which to make their voices heard. Thus at the 2001 Stockholm International Forum on

British skinheads protesting the arrival of Romani refugees from the Czech Republic, 1990s.

Combatting Intolerance, the Romani representative was not included in the program's closing session during which the different national delegates presented their summaries and agendas. The reason given for being left out was that "the Romani people don't have a country or a govern- ment". When Czechoslovakia was being constituted in 1918, its cri- terion for recognising its various ethnic minorities rested upon whether they were represented by a nation state or not. Thus the ethnic Hungarians, for example, qualified because of the existence of the neighboring country of Hungary, but Romanies did not, despite being one of the largest minority populations in Czechoslovakia, because there was no Romani homeland. Indeed, had more been known then about our origins in India, and if Indian administrators had been approached for intervention, things might be dif- ferent today. After all, it was India which helped spon- sor the First World Romani Congress in Britain in 1971 and which was instrumental in the achievement of Romani representation at the United Nations.

Physical appearance

Crabb (1832:10) wrote that "it is remarkable that, when they first came into Europe, they were black, and that the women were still blacker than the men" while Grellmann before him (1783:10) described Romanies as "black horrid men … the dark brown or olive coloured skin of the Gipseys, with their white teeth appearing between their red lips, may be a disgusting sight to an European, unaccustomed to such objects". The Church also viewed negatively the appearance of the first Romanies,

because mediaeval Christian doc-
trine associated light with purity
and darkness with sin. The earliest church records documenting
the arrival of Romanies alluded to
the swarthiness of their complexion and the inherent evil which
that supposedly demonstrated:
"[t]he conviction that blackness
denotes inferiority and evil [was]
well rooted in the western mind.
The nearly black skins of many
Gypsies marked them out to be
victims of this prejudice" (Kenrick and Puxon, 1972:19).
Hobson expanded upon this
(quoted in Dunstan, 1965:338):

Straffe der Ziegeuner, Juden
Vetter und Landstreicher.

Association with darkness and
dirt is a convenient hook on which
to hang certain projections, especially if [the target] is a
relatively unknown visitor from a far-off country with a
strange culture, or if he threatens important economic
and other social, vested interests. He is also clearly 'not
me'. While the association between darkness and evil
is a purely metaphorical one, its effects have been
devastating.

Seventeenth and nine-
teenth century placards
showing a traditional punishment for Romanies who
trespassed within city
limits: flogging with a
bundle of reeds.

Philip Mason (1968:61) has emphasised that "hardly any white man has
overcome the confusion between biological accident and symbolic
metaphor". Dark skin was much more a factor 700 years ago than it is
today. The early Romanies' identity as non-white, heathen outsiders
became incorporated into Christian European folklore, which only served
to institutionalise and encourage the prejudice against them. Like
Asahuerus, the Jew doomed to wander throughout eternity because he
refused to allow Jesus to rest in his doorway while on his way to Calvary,
Romanies were accused of forging the nails with which Christ was
crucified. And while Jews were accused of drinking the blood of Christian babies in hidden rites to which no outsider was allowed access,
Romanies were likewise charged with stealing and even eating those

A Dutch placard ordering the deaths of Romanies entering the territory. The Netherlands, 1726.

babies. Paralleling even more closely the Asahuerus myth is the belief that the original sin of the Romanies was their refusal to give Mary and the baby Jesus shelter during their flight from King Herod into Egypt.

Exclusionary culture

Romani culture, called *Rromanìja* or *Rromanipe* or *Rromipe*, does not encourage close social relationships with non-Romani populations (this is explained in Chapter 7). Behaving in an exclusivist way can easily lead to an assumption on the part of those who are 'left out' that such a group is secretive, and must be hiding something. The maintenance of cultural and/or religious restrictions that keep outsiders at a distance must certainly be seen as one major historical factor accounting for both antigypsyism and antisemitism. The need to keep the non-Romani population at arm's length has also prevented investigators from gaining too intimate an acquaintance with the Romani world, which has led to highly embellished and stereotyped published accounts. These in turn have kept alive the 'otherness' and distance of Romanies, both of which factors have helped sustain a literary or fantasy image, and which have worked very effectively against Romani issues being taken seriously.

Exclusion works in the other direction too. The wall built in Ústí nad Labem in the Czech Republic in 1999 to separate Romanies from the rest of the town, or the ghetto which Mayor Ion Rotaru of Piatra Neamţ in Romania announced in 2001 that he would create on the site of a former chicken farm for that town's Romani inhabitants, were both intended to exclude us from the rest of the community.

Our way of life

Because of laws forbidding Romanies to settle, which began to be passed soon after our arrival in Europe, means of livelihood had to be relied upon which could be easily and quickly gathered up when it became necessary to move out of an area when the law demanded. One such means was fortune telling, but this only

Marksman's target used at the Frenštát pod Radhoštěm rifle club in Bohemia between 1839 and 1900, depicting a Romani couple.

helped reinforce the image of mystery and exoticism that was growing in the European mind. Romanies, in turn, have exploited this image as a means of protection since one is less likely to show hostility towards a person whom one believes to have some measure of control over, or knowledge of, one's destiny. The fact that Romanies are in some sense an Asian population in Europe who speak an Asian language that serves as the vehicle of a culture and world-view originating in Asia, has also created conflict. Fortune telling is a highly regarded profession in India, for example, but not in Europe; begging is likewise viewed very differently in Hindu and Islamic societies, where giving alms to beggars is a religious obligation; but it has no such special status in the West today.

A frequent charge made against us is that we have too many children. This is not because birth control is carelessly disregarded as is usually claimed, but because just as in India, our children are seen as our fortune.

The public torture of
Romanies in Giessen,
Germany, 1727.

A common saying in Romani is *but čhave but baxt*
("many children much luck"). Our children help with
earning income and keeping it in the family – also one
of the reasons why we might not keep them at school
for long.

Some aspects of Romani culture are so distinct from those of the
European societies that they have, at times, been regarded as their very
antithesis; as Kephart (1982:43) has said, "if people perceive of Gypsies
as a counterculture, then unfortunately for all concerned, prejudice and
discrimination might be looked upon as justifiable retaliation". An editorial by Matthew Braham that appeared in the British newspaper *The
Guardian* on 8 April 2000, stated that:

> The Roma are perhaps the most singularly disliked ethnic group in the
> world … the Roma too are part of the problem, through the persistence of
> a culture that is as much a source of their marginalization as is the major-
> ity prejudice against them.

Guenther Lewy also believes we are to blame for our problems: "prejudice alone", he wrote, "is not sufficient explanation for the hostility
directed at Gypsies … certain characteristics of Gypsy life tend to reinforce or even create hostility" (2000:213). Not only does our culture
create this prejudice, according to his point of view, but we are apparently also responsible for fanning the flames of xenophobia ourselves:
"prejudice and discrimination have not disappeared, being kept alive

especially by the large influx of Gypsies from Eastern Europe" (Lewy, 2000:11).

Some of the "characteristics" that Lewy refers to are simply misinterpretations of Romani culture, but they can inadvertently lead to discrimination nevertheless. The author was contacted for advice by a hospital in San Francisco in 1995, where a young father who was saying a prayer for his newborn daughter had been overheard by a nurse. She thought that our word *Devla*, which means "oh God", was the English word "devil" and she reported him as a satanist. Accusations of cannibalism have been made because the phrases we use for "please", mean "I eat your heart", or "I eat your liver" (*xav tj'o ilo, xav tj'o buko*), even though the same expressions are found in Hungarian. Both Grellman (1783) and Serboianu (1930) wrote about our supposed taste for human flesh!

Slaves being led to the Giessen mass torture, 1727.

The parallel, created 'gypsy' image

As Okely has pointed out, "outsiders have projected onto Gypsies their own repressed fantasies and longings for disorder" (1983:232; see also Sibley, 1981:195–6), and they have at the same time used those imagined characteristics of the small-*g* 'gypsy' as a yardstick by which to measure the boundaries of their own identities. Thus an individual's occasional urge to challenge the establishment, or to engage in some anti-social act, or even his subconscious fascination with anarchy are, as psychologists recognise, not likely ever to be realised by that individual, though they can be experienced vicariously or subliminally by being projected onto the 'outlaw' Romani population. This phenomenon is reflected repeatedly in the media as well as in works of fiction. Since the nineteenth century, a literary 'gypsy', (always written with a lower-case 'g') has emerged, which is presented as the epitome of freedom: freedom from responsibility, freedom from moral constraints, freedom from the requirements of hygiene, freedom from nine-to-five routine. This has remained unchallenged by the Romani community because while it was becoming established as a part of the western world-view, Romanies were unaware of its emergence. By the time the Romani community began to react and object, it was too late. We have also lacked access to the traditional means necessary to combat stereotyping, such as law suits, or organised boycotting, or write-in campaigns, and thus there has grown in the popular mind an image which combines fascination with resentment, even with repulsion, and which is steadily fueled by novelists and journalists (dealt with in Chapter 6). As Janos Kenedi has noted, because of their reliance in large measure upon literary and poorly researched sources for their background information on Romanies, "the mass media, in a veiled and often less-veiled form, goad opinion in an anti-Gypsy direction" (1986:14).

Scapegoatism

The fact that we have no military, political, economic and (particularly) territorial strength, and no nation state to speak for us, ensures that we are an ideal target for scapegoatism, or easy blame. Beck (1985:103) has made this point very well in referring to the situation of our people in Romania:

> Romania's German-speaking populations have received support from the West German state. Magyars are supported by the Hungarian state, and Jews by Israel. Groups such as the Gypsies do not have such an advantage. Lacking a protective state, they have no one to turn to when discrimination is inflicted upon them as a group. Unlike ethnic groups represented by states, Gypsies are not recognised as having a history that could legitimize them.

Further to these observations on scapegoatism, it has been argued, by e.g. Kenedi, that there is a need in all societies to select groups upon which to blame its problems. Those least able to defend themselves provide the best targets. And if Romanies are "here today and gone tomorrow", what better evidence that they are guilty and are fleeing from the scene?

The vague understanding of Romani origins

In the above quote Beck states that we are "not recognised as having a history that could legitimize" us. Others have written that we have no history at all; one recent study begins with the words "[t]he Gypsies are a people without a history, and therefore without an identity" (Glase, 1998:1). Countries place great emphasis on their histories and commemorate and glorify them with national holidays, anthems, monuments and parades. But in the Romani case, our history is vague. We ourselves have forgotten it and the non-Romani scholars have presented a great many confusing theories of their own about us; the result is that people don't know who we really are, and we aren't yet in a position to tell them. Fonseca (1996:100) commented that our "ambiguous origins" have allowed us to "be whoever [we] want to be". This is what has in fact happened, though not so much on our part as on the part of those writing about us: we are whatever they want us to be, and in the absence of a well-recognised history and clearly understood ethnic identity, our whole presence as a people remains in a sense confusing. When we are left out of discussions, or passed over in matters of legislative decision-making, it is not always deliberate; it is often simply because our identity and – particularly – our representation, seems vague. Combined with our lack of political influence or a loud voice, we are very easily overlooked. We seem only to matter when we become associated with other people's problems.

In sum, then, we can seek the historical basis of anti-Romani prejudice in a number of areas, in particular racism, religious intolerance, outsider status and the fact that Romanies maintain an exclusionary or separatist culture. In large part too, the literary image of the 'gypsy' blurs the distinction between the real and the imagined population, so that even factual reports of antigypsyism seldom receive the concern they deserve. All of these factors underlie the problems that face the Romani populations throughout the world today.

Questions

1 Antigypsyism is the cumulation of several different factors over time. What are they?
2 What is *racism*?
3 Is *race* a meaningful concept?
4 What is *ethnicity*? Do you belong to an ethnic group?
5 How does institutionalized racism differ from personal racism?
6 Have you encountered any instances of antigypsyism recently? If so, describe and discuss.
7 Why did people think Romanies were cannibals?

CHAPTER SIX

The Gypsy image

Use of the word *gypsy* to convey an image rather than identify an actual individual is very common indeed. Many novels and films that include small-*g* 'gypsies' don't give them personal or family names – they are simply images meant to add colour, though not usually plot development, to the story. 'Gypsy', and its equivalents in other languages, has come to stand for anyone following a particular way of life, especially one that involves travelling about or living outside the law. Thus in English there are 'gypsy scholars', 'gypsy preachers', 'gypsy taxis' and so on. One children's storybook is called *Rama the Gypsy Cat*, and the cat is a 'gypsy' because it wears an earring and has no home.

This fictional image originates in the idealizing of the western European Romani populations during the period of the industrial revolution, when they came to symbolize in literature an earlier idyllic, rural way of life. This coincided with European concepts of the 'noble savage', and the realisation that there were heathen populations living in the heart of civilisation in desperate need of Christian salvation. The early Victorian period saw the appearance of several works on missionary activity amongst Romanies (Mayall, 1988).

Origins of the fictionalized Gypsy

Over 130 years ago, Simson (1865:8) called the fictitious image of the Romani as wanderer "very erroneous", and pointed out that "nomadic Gypsies constitute but a portion of the race, and a very small portion of it". Okely has made a similar point: "Gypsies do not travel about aimlessly, as either the romantics or the anti-Gypsy suggest" (1983:125). Semi-scholarly treatments of Romanies are numerous and readily available, and lack of information cannot be the reason for the perpetuation of the myths surrounding us. But the *idea* that a lack of information exists has itself become a part of that myth. We must look for the reasons for its persistence elsewhere.

THE GIPSY'S LIFE IS A JOYOUS LIFE,

A songsheet from 1850 depicting the pastoral image of Gypsy life.

The contemporary, created 'gypsy' persona is the result of a dynamic which got out of hand in the last century and which then took on a life of its own. It was stimulated by a combination of the responses to industrialization, colonialism and emerging nineteenth century ideas of racial hierarchy.

As mills, mines, factories and rail transportation transformed the land, so perceptions of the pre-industrial, rural world of the earlier century acquired a magical quality that was promoted in the poems and paintings of the mid-1800s. This nostalgia idealized the world of the farmer and the shepherd and of rural life; Romanies were seen as the ultimate symbols of this vanishing world, a remote population unspoilt by civilisation, content to live in and off the fields and forests. Meanwhile, western European powers were claiming large areas of the non-white world, and becoming increasingly powerful and influential. Technology was seen as a mark of civilisation, although Eastern societies viewed the West as spiritually backward. Writers of the age such as Darwin, Gobineau and Knox produced scientific studies ranking human groups in terms of their 'advancement' and 'development'. These were based upon classifications originating in the new disciplines of botany and zoology but were now increasingly being applied to human categories. The notion that some 'races' were more highly developed than others, and that some of them exhibited 'mixed' developmental characteristics due to genetic interbreeding – always seen as having negative consequences – gave rise to the ideas both of racial purity and racial degradation. From here it was but a short jump to establishing the identity of the 'True Romany', i.e. the individual who fit the epitomized

"King of the Gypsies"
theatre-style, although there
is no royalty in traditional
Romani social structure.

persona, who caused no trouble, who had no interest in getting involved in mainstream society, who lived safely at a distance on fruit and wild animals, and the occasional vegetables stolen from the farmers' fields, and who stayed with his own kind. This became flesh and blood in the fiction and (increasingly) the non-fiction of the era, and is still with us today. Semi-academic societies were established, predictably having no Romani members, and sometimes having the saving of the Gypsy soul as their goal; journals appeared in which the genealogies of Romani families (called 'pedigrees' as though the subjects were cocker spaniels) were published, and articles glorifying and glamorizing the *True Romany*. This approach allowed writers and policy-makers to dismiss those who didn't qualify as being an unwelcome social blot on the land, people of mixed 'Romani blood' who gave the *True Romany* a bad name, though in fact such people constitute the entirety of the actual Romani population. A millennium after leaving India as an already-mixed people, there are no Romanies anywhere in the world – just as there are no non-Romani populations anywhere – who are genetically pristine. The concept itself is in any case unproductive and unscientific, but it laid the foundation for racial policies that, in the twentieth century, led to the attempted extermination of the entire Romani population in Europe in the *Porrajmos* (Chapter 4).

While the misrepresentation of ethnic and social groups eventually comes to be challenged by members of those groups, this did not begin to happen in the case of Romanies until very recently. Being an essentially powerless and unschooled population, few were even aware of the Romani golem coming to life in the world of the *gadže*. Visitors with notebooks showing up in Romani homes were nothing new, and the social distance between themselves and the Romanies they were intruding upon assured their seldom being asked to leave. They were told what they expected to hear, particularly if they were paying for information, in an attempt to get them to leave as soon as possible. That they were provided with misleading information is evident simply by reading what they have written; it is clear that, in the absence of fact or detail, such writers and researchers supplied it from their own imaginations. Both Romani protective behaviour, and the non-Romani responses to it, continue today. Perhaps this stand-off has become too deeply entrenched ever to be completely eradicated. One disturbing aspect is that very many of these misleading presentations of Romanies turn up in children's books, and are read at the very time when attitudes and stereotypes about other populations are being formed.

The two faces of Romani identity

Most people still get their information about Romanies from books rather than from first-hand experience. A surprising number still don't believe that we even really exist. In response to a request sent to *The Daily Texan* newspaper (for 8 March 1975) asking that 'gypsy' be written with a proper noun's capital letter, its editor wrote that "[a] lower-case *g* will continue to be used, for the simple reason that gypsies are a contrived people and not a legitimate ethnic group". The same paper reiterated that position a decade later in 1985 after a reader criticised the use of the slang word 'gyp' to mean 'cheat' in an article. The printed reply was that "'gyp' is not an ethnic slur, for the simple reason that gypsies are not an actual people". More recently, and for just the same reason, a letter which appeared in the *Anchorage Daily News* (in 1999) condemning the same use of 'gyp' in a headline drew a number of follow-up letters from the readers. One said:

> Perhaps [the writer] does not know that the word 'gyp' deriving from 'gypsy' is not the least bit a racial slur. Gypsies do not imply a race or ethnicity, but rather a nomadic lifestyle.

And another argued:

> [The writer] states that the term 'gyp' was a racial term that offends Gypsies. Now correct me if I'm wrong, but aren't racial slurs supposed to be offensive towards a race? Last time I checked, Gypsies weren't a race, but a rather unique lifestyle.

As long as we are seen as a people defined only by behaviour, then the idea will persist that we can stop being 'gypsies' simply by changing it, the way hippies could choose to stop being hippies or hobos could stop being hobos. Unless we as a real people are taken seriously, then our real-life situation will never be taken seriously.

Romani reaction to treatment by non-Romanies has taken two main directions. On the one hand there has been a withdrawal from all unnecessary social and physical contact with *gadže*. Cultural pressures to remain separate have existed since the exodus out of India, and no doubt have their origins in the Indian caste system, being subsequently reinforced by imposed exclusionism. Among contemporary Romani populations the way these pressures work differs from group to group, being most strongly maintained by those who descend from the liberated slaves. But Romani children everywhere are taught from the beginning that a clear division exists between people who are Romanies and people who are not. While this seems to be more rigorously maintained in places where antigypsyism is greater, it is nevertheless reinforced everywhere by notions of cleanliness, eating habits, the handling of animals, sexual behaviour and so on (dealt with in Chapter 7). The desirability of being a Romani is emphasized; and, while there are no illusions about the difficulties of maintaining Romani moral and cultural values in a non-Romani environment, few Romanies believe that those of you non-Romanies are superior. At the same time, great lengths are gone to in order to protect the ethnic identity; it is still the case that only a handful of Romanies admit their ethnicity publicly if they are able to hide it. On the other hand, there has also been an internalization of the stereotype, and it has sometimes been given right back to the public that created it in the first place, the rationale being that if this is what fascinates them, and if they are even willing to pay for it, then let them have it.

Negative media attention can also harm the whole community. Police will step up their harassment of all Romanies in an area, even when just one individual or family is under investigation. Nevertheless, an image can also come from within the Romani community itself intentionally to mislead the public, as a means of self-protection. In the same way, outsiders are discouraged from learning the Romani language and may be told that it is Greek or Spanish (see Chapter 14). It is believed that if inquisitive non-Romanies are busy pursuing the myth, they will leave the real thing alone, but while the myth serves as an insulation that allows a minimum of interference from outside, it also hinders interaction which could be useful.

Questions

1 Where does the 'gypsy image' come from?
2 Why is it so persistent, even though information on the real population is readily available?
3 Do Romanies themselves help to sustain an inaccurate 'gypsy image'?

CHAPTER SEVEN

How Indian are Romanies?

"Oh Indra, determine who are Aryan and who are Dasa, and separate them!"

Hindu saying

While a nine centuries' removal from India has diluted the Indian biological connection to the extent that for some Romani groups it may hardly be representative today, Sareen (1976:42) concluded that overall, we still remain closer, genetically, to Asians than to the Europeans around us; European genetic material, for some groups at least, is still located at the shallow end of the gene pool:

> The European Gypsies, who migrated from Northern India about 800-1,000 years ago, have been well studied serologically, mostly by ABO, MNS and Rh systems. The results indicate that their blood groups agree well with the warrior classes of northern India ... and differ significantly from those of the local European population ... the individuality of the blood its other serum protein factors, such as haptoglobins, transferins, the group-specific component (Gc) and the Gm system. Hp1 gene has been known to be the least common in Asia, with a gene frequency of only 0.2 to 0.3; it could thus help in studies on Roma. Haptoglobin groups have been studied in Swedish Gypsies in comparison with those in Swedes and North Indians, and these also point to their North Indian origin.

Siváková (1983:98), another geneticist who has compared Indian, Romani and European serological material, found the same results:

> As can be seen, the lowest genetic distance value was found between the recent Indian population and the Slovak Gypsies. In other words, these two populations are in the closest relationship, suggesting a relatively low degree of genetic assimilation of Gypsies with their surrounding populations.

Mastana and Papiha (1992:50) have demonstrated that this is more evident in eastern European Romani populations than among those in western Europe, where the incidence of mixing with non-Romanies has been higher:

> The evidence of the present study favours that Gypsy populations of eastern Europe still have greater genetic affinity with Indian nomadic groups and the genetic differentiation may primarily be due to isolation, high rate of migration of subgroups towards Europe and genetic drift, whilst the Western Gypsies are more homogeneous to their local population which might have resulted from a high degree of genetic admixture.

"Mum, is it true that Gypsies are of Asiatic origin?"

The mother's expression in this cartoon reflects the scepticism of some Romanies on learning of our Indian origin.

Nevertheless, culture, language and identity are not inherited genetically but socially, and apart from the genetic and linguistic evidence, a core of direct, unbroken transmission from India in these other areas may also be readily identified. While there are many Romani customs and beliefs for which no origin has been determined (such as symbolically cutting the invisible *lupunza* or fetters which tie an infant's feet together to allow it to learn to walk), further parallels in India may yet be found as research continues.

Some would seem to be incontrovertibly Indian, however. These are found among Romanies throughout the world in all areas of the culture; some groups in Hungary, Slovakia and Transylvania maintain the Indian bhairava musical scale, for example, as well as a type of mouth music known in India as *bōl* and called *bega* in Romani (and *szaj bögö* in Hungarian), which consists of nonsense syllables imitating the rhythm of the tabla drum. The tribunal where internal disputes are settled, called the *kris(i)* in Romani – a Greek word – has the same form and function as the Indian *panchayat* or *nasab*, or with the earlier administrative and judicial Rajput body of men called the *panchakāla* from which the panchayat developed. The *pilivani* wrestling matches with oiled bodies, called

Burning possessions at a
funeral, among Romanies in
Britain (left) and Germany
(right).

pehlivān in India and Iran, and stick dancing (called
rovljako khelipe or *botolo* in Romani) are both still
found amongst Romanies in Hungary; snake-charm-
ing (called *farmeko sapano*) is a profession among
Romanies in Serbia; the burning of one's possessions
after death (called *phabaripe*) and even (among some populations at least
into the twentieth century) the ritual suicide of the widow has striking
parallels with *sāti* in India. Marriages (*biava*) which are arranged by the
couple's families (the betrothals are called *thomnimata*), and which take
place between children, and which involve dowry (*darro*), are Romani as
well as Indian. Fonseca (1996:110–11) has commented upon the Romani
habit found in India of "shaking the head from side to side to signify
'yes'".

Hübschmannová (1972) provides valuable insights into the parallels
between traditional Indian social structure and the divisions within
Rromanipen. She has also found (1978:277–8) what she believes to be
retentions of Indian personal names among Romanies in the Czech
Republic. Some of these, which existed among the *adivasi* subcaste are
Bado, Dužda, Gadžor, Goral, Kanči, Karela and *Mirga*, and are all found
in Europe today. Rishi (1976) lists several more that he has also recognised as Indian.

Some Romani groups in Europe today appear to maintain elements of
Shaktism or goddess-worship; the Rajputs worshipped the warrior-
goddess *Parvati*, another name for the female deity *Sāti-Sara*, who is
identified with Saint Sarah, the Romani Goddess of Fate. That she forms
part of the yearly pilgrimage to La Camargue at Stes. Maries de la Mer in
the south of France is of particular significance; here she is carried into

the sea just as she is carried into the waters of the Ganges each December in India. Both Sāti-Sara and St Sarah wear a crown, both are also called *Kali*, and both have shining faces painted black. Sāti-Sara is a consort of the god *Śiva*, and is known by many other names, *Bhadrakāli*, *Umā*, *Durgā* and *Syamā* among them. Like some other Romani cultural practices, this is no doubt a syncretism of both Asian and European customs. Various Romani populations in Europe and America also maintain *nacijange semnura* or group symbols, such as the sun (representing the Serbian Romanies) and the moon (representing the Lovara), which may be found drawn or carved onto the *stago* or 'standard' at a wedding, and on the *semno* or *rupuni rovli* ('silver baton'), i.e. the clan leader's staff, and which are appealed to at the consecration of the *mulengi sinija* or 'table of the dead' at a Vlax Romani *pomana* (plural *pomeni*) or wake. Here, the invocation is *"Khama, Čhona thaj Devla, ašun man!"* which means "Sun, Moon and God, hear me". The signifi-

Statue of *E Sara e Kali*, La Camargue, southern France.

cance is in the fact that the Sun and the Moon were the two symbols worn emblematically on the armour and tunics of the Rajput warriors to identify them in battle from all others.

Elements of an Indian legacy have been preserved in Romani riddles. Reference to the Vedic god of the wind and the air, *Vayu* (also called *Marut*), is retained in a number of these: *Kana hulavel peske bal o Vajo, legenisavol e čar* ("When Vayu combs his hair, the grass sways"), *Amaro Vajo hurjal tela savorrenge podji, aj konik našti t'astarel les* ("Our Vayu flies under everyone's petticoats, and no one can catch him"), *O pharo vurdon e Vajosko cirdajlo ekhe šele grastendar kaj phurden ande'l rrutunja* ("Vayu's heavy waggon is pulled by a hundred horses blowing through their nostrils") – the answer to each is *e balval* "the wind". In Indian theology the task of Vayu's son *Māruti* (also called *Hanuman*) is to tear open the clouds and let the rain fall, and in Romani the expression *marutisjol o Del* means "the sky [*lit*. "God"] is growing overcast". The reference to a hundred horses may also be of Vedic origin; there are several references in the scriptures to the *aśvamedha yajña* or "horse sacrifice", whereby in ancient India the king would release one hundred horses to roam freely through his kingdom. Stopping them or blocking their path was forbidden.

The female spirits or fates, called the *vursitorja*, hover in its presence three days after a child is born to determine its destiny and to influence the choice of name the parents will decide upon. They may be compared with the Indian *mātrkā* or 'little mother' spirits who also possess a baby's destiny at the time of its birth. The red thread (the *loli dori*) tied around a newborn's ankle or wrist and worn for two or three years after-wards to guard against the *jakhalo* or 'evil eye' reflects the protective properties of that colour, which is also worn or painted on the body in India. Such customs are found among Baltic Romani groups as well as among Vlax Romanies.

Śiva's trident, called *triśula* in Sanskrit, changed its role from Hindu symbol to Christian symbol and has become the Romani word for "cross" (*trušul*). This probably happened when the migration first reached Armenia; in the Lomavren language *terusul* means both "church" and "priest", another indication that the ancestors of the Rom and the Lom may still have been together at that time. Similarly, *rašaj* "(Christian) holy man" represents a shift of meaning from Sanskrit *ārseya* "of a (Hindu) holy man". The Romani word for "Easter", *Patradji*, as well as the word *kirvo* "godfather" are almost certainly from Armenian, as is the word *xanamik*, "co-parent-in-law", further indication that it was in Armenian-speaking lands that our ancestors first encoun-tered Christianity. Although Hinduism as a cohesive faith has not sur-vived – our people today practicing a great number of religions adopted because of a historical need to survive – nevertheless many beliefs remi-niscent of Hinduism continue in day-to-day cultural behaviour. These similarities have been discussed in a number of works by Indian authors, among them Rishi, Joshi, Bhattacharya, Lal, Shashi and Singhal, and these can be usefully read for more parallels between Romani and Indian societies.

'Religion' is usually thought of in terms of a physical place of wor-ship, a clergy and a set of written scriptures, and for this reason it has been repeatedly stated that since we have none of these, we must there-fore have no religion of our own. It has historically been the case too that a people's religion forms part and parcel of its identity, and every medieval nation guarded its own brand of Orthodoxy or Islam. The claim that we lacked this most fundamental characteristic of 'peoplehood' has served to place us yet further beyond the boundaries of ordered and civilised society. One story maintains that we did have a church once long ago, but it was made of cheese and we got hungry and ate it.

A truer definition of religion is that it is the belief in a higher spiritual power, and the maintenance of a daily way of life dedicated to serving and pleasing that power. From this perspective, not only do we have a religion, but living it is so much a part of our lives that we don't even think of it as such; it isn't only saved for the weekends. We believe in one god, *o Devel* or *o Del*, and the devil, *o Beng*, and we believe that there is a constant struggle between them for dominance over our lives. To live properly is to abide by a set of behaviours collectively called *Rroma-nipen*, *Rromipe* or *Rromanija*, and this entails maintaining spiritual balance. This Ayurvedic concept, called *karma* in India (and in Romani *kintala*, or in some dialects *kintari* or *kintujmos*) is fundamental to the Romani worldview. Such a dualistic perspective groups the universe into pairs, God and the Devil, Romanies and non-Romanies, adults and children, clean and polluted – even the stages of life are two in number: adulthood (when one is able to produce children) and, together, childhood and old age (when one is not able to produce children).

Time spent in the non-Romani world (the *jado*) drains spiritual energy or *dji*. Sampson (1926:257) gives the various meanings of this word as "[s]eat of the emotions, heart, soul; temper, disposition, mood; courage, spirit", comparing it to Sanskrit *jīva*, Hindi *jī*, "life, soul, spirit, mind" and Armenian (*h*)*ogi*, "soul". One's spiritual batteries can only be recharged by spending time in an all-Romani environment – in the normal course of events, in family homes. It is in this area of spiritual and physical wellbeing (*baxt*) that the Indian origin of our Romani people is most clearly seen.

In the preparation of food, and in one's personal hygiene and deportment, it is absolutely essential that a separation between the two conditions of 'pure' and 'polluted' be sustained. A pure state is achieved by maintaining the spiritual balance in one's life and avoiding shame (*ladžav* or *ladž*); that is, being declared unclean or, in extreme cases, being shunned by the community. Avoiding shame involves, among other things, demonstrating *patjiv* or 'respect' to the elders. Maintaining balance or harmony pleases the spirits of the ancestors (the *mulé*), and they are there to guard one and help one to do it, but if they are displeased, they will mete out punishment, or a 'warning signal' (*prikaza*), by way of retribution. Depending upon the nature of the transgression, this may be mild, e.g. stubbing one's toe, or so severe as to involve sickness and even death. The consequences of *prikaza* underlie the universal Romani belief that nothing is an accident – that nothing happens simply by chance.

The penalty for extreme pollution is being banished, or made an outcast, and an out-caste, from the community, for which different Romani words are *durjardo*, *gonime* or *stražime*. 'Banishment' is variously *durjaripe*, *gonimos* or *straža*, which may or may not imply a state of pollution, being imposed also for other reasons, e.g. disregard for territorial claims. Being in a state of pollution is being *magerdo*, *marime*, *pokhelime* or *makherdo* (literally 'smeared', i.e. with menstrual blood). These words can be contrasted with *melalo* which also means 'dirty', but only from physical dirt. *Daravipe* ('fearfulness', from *dar* 'fear') is a particular charge of marital infidelity that, if proven, also demands a penalty, perhaps even the disfigurement of the offending party.

Prikaza brings bad luck (*bibaxt*) and illness (*nasvalipe*), and it can be attracted even by socializing with people who are not *vuže* (< *vužo* 'clean'). Non-Romani people are seen as not being *vuže*, which is why Romanies avoid intimate contact with them. But this is not an inherited condition of non-Romanies, it is because these cultural practices are not maintained. A non-Romani woman who marries into a Romani family is expected to adopt them, and in doing so becomes in that context *vuži*. Without a doubt, it is particularly the factor of ritual cleanliness and ritual defilement that has helped maintain Romani separateness – and as a result Romani identity – for so long.

Questions

1 How have modern genetic studies helped to confirm the Indian origin of Romanies?
2 List five aspects of modern Romani culture that point to an Indian origin.
3 Is there a danger that the 'Indianness' of Romanies could be exaggerated or exploited? Discuss.
4 Is there a danger in emphasising this in today's Europe?
5 How would you define 'religion'? Could the Romanies' interpretation of a dualistic universe be seen as their religion?

CHAPTER EIGHT

How European are Romanies?

Why do the Roma have to be recognised as a 'European' or even a 'truly European' minority, as in the Brussels Declaration of 1996? Some Romani intellectuals and leaders recall the Roma's Indian origin and heritage as a basis for their political status and identity, while others eagerly affirm their European roots and heritage and consider their Indian past as irrelevant to the current Romani causes and claims.

(Mirga and Gheorghe, 1997:22)

Šaip Jusuf, noted Yugoslav Romani linguist and litterateur (addressing the 1976 Roma seminar in India) said his feeling of affinity with India was so intense that he refused to call his people 'gypsy' or to recognise their belonging to any European country

(Sharma, 1976:29-30)

In a very real sense, we are as European as anyone else. 'European' isn't a nationality or an ethnicity; Europeans are composed of a multitude of these. 'European' doesn't mean being originally from a part of Europe; if that were true, the Saami and Hungarians and Finns and Estonians wouldn't be 'Europeans'. Having a country isn't a qualification; if that were true then the Basques, the Catalans and the Frisians wouldn't qualify. Only a few years ago in the context of the European Union, there were discussions in the London press about whether the *British* were 'Europeans' or not.

So what makes a European? It is a state of mind, a sense of belonging to a part of the world and being a part of its history and its different regional and ethnic cultures. In all of these, Romanies are in no way different from other peoples inhabiting Europe. Indeed, it might be argued

A Romani cartoon from the Czech Republic reflecting the fear *gadže* have of Gypsies.

that we are *quintessentially* European, being found in all of its countries like no other single European people; the first section of Will Guy's *Between Past and Future: The Roma of Central and Eastern Europe* (2001) is entitled "A Truly European People," while in Mirga and Gheorghe's *Roma in the Twenty-First Century* (1997), which is devoted in large part to the question of identity, the above quote is its sole acknowledgment of an Indian connection.

While the knowledge of our Indian origins is important, just as it is important for any nation to know its own history, it is not a body of knowledge that is kept in mind on a daily basis. In fact most Romanies don't even know about it. Some of us don't believe it when we first hear about it. When skinheads carry placards which say "Gypsies Go Back To India" this is an informed but unrealistic bigotry – European Romanies regard Europe as home, not India. Our own spokesmen who believe we should refrain from bringing too much attention to our Indian connection argue that if we stress our non-Europeanness, it will merely serve as justification for those who would like us to leave. And in any case, in light of the details about our history which are now emerging, we may not even have begun to be an ethnic population *until* our ancestors reached the West, and the time spent in Europe and beyond accounts for practically the entirety of the Romani experience.

However, being European means sharing a common sense of identity, and recognising each other as equally 'European'. A public opinion poll which was conducted in Kremnica, Slovakia, in 1993 revealed that while 100 per cent of the Romani respondents said "yes" to the question "Should Roma live together with Slovaks and have the same living conditions as Slovaks have", 91 per cent of the Slovaks who responded said "no". Other such polls conducted in other countries sadly reveal similar responses. Romanies can only be Europeans if Europeans want them to be – if they are willing to open the door and let Romanies in – and so far, this doesn't seem to be happening.

Despite the emphasis on Europe, it is important to remember that we are a diaspora people found all over the world; we are a *global* population, with between a quarter and a third of our total number found *outside* of that part of the world. The exclusive focusing of Romani-related organisations on populations only located in Europe fails to acknowledge our existence internationally. With the constant (especially post-communist) migration of members of European Romani families to North and South America and to Australia, and with the tremendous increase in the use of the internet, contacts linking us around the world will continue to grow.

Questions

1 What is a 'European'? What makes *you* one?
2 "Romanies are not Europeans" – discuss.
3 "Romanies are the true Europeans" – discuss.

CHAPTER NINE

Cuisine

Like Romani music, there is no single type of Romani cookery, but a range of cuisines that differ from place to place, depending upon locally available ingredients and the social circumstances of the community. But, also like Romani music, whatever that local diet consists of, it will have a distinctively Romani touch to it, usually in the seasonings used. Savoury Romani dishes are typically considered to be peppery, and there is some truth to this since both red and black pepper are 'auspicious' seasonings (discussed below); even commercially produced 'Gypsy' dishes, such as Knorr Swiss' *Zigeunerschnitzel* seasoning or their *Sos Cigánski* are only distinctive because they contain cayenne pepper. In other places on the other hand, it is skin colour which seems to add a 'gypsy' distinctiveness. In Britain, McVitie markets a brand of cookies called 'Gypsy Creams' and Jacob's sells its 'Romany Creams', both are brown sandwich biscuits with a brown creme filling. In Italy, Bonbonetti produces both 'Gipsy boy' and 'Gipsy Lady' wafers, which are covered in chocolate. Predictably this is not the connection in the United States, where a tisane called 'Gypsy Cold Care' relies instead on the 'natural folk medicine' stereotype. Needless to say, chocolate cookies and Wienerschnitzl are not real, traditional Romani fare, but it would be a mistake to believe that Romanies who enjoy them are betraying the culture!

In eastern Europe, where the population has been sedentary for centuries, the dishes are very much like those eaten by the surrounding non-Romanies; 'Romani tea', for example, is the same as Russian tea, and *sarmi*, cabbage rolls, are also found in plenty of European ethnic cultures under different names. In western Europe, where Romani groups have been more mobile, choice of diet has for centuries depended upon what was available directly from the land. Game animals and birds, such as rabbits, hares, quail and partridge are well represented; hedgehogs and snails are also traditional sources of food among central and western European Romani groups. For some Romani populations, Romanichals in Britain for instance, speaking the names of certain animals aloud (sometimes ever, sometimes only any time before noon) is considered to attract bad luck, and euphemisms are used, such as 'longtail' or 'wriggler'. About the only things not eaten are animals with unclean habits: dogs and cats, for example, which clean their own bodies. Horses cannot lick their hindquarters and are therefore not contaminated animals, but such is their significance in Romani culture, that the idea of eating horse-meat is shocking to us. During the years following the Second World War when horsemeat was readily available, many Romanies preferred to go hungry rather than eat it. Today, some refugees among our people are facing such miserable conditions of hunger that they are obliged to break some of these cultural restrictions just to stay alive.

Something should be said about the oft-repeated assertion that we eat carrion. This is not wildlife salvaged for food that has been freshly killed in e.g. a road accident, but anything that has been dead for some time and is in a state of decomposition. Romanies have certainly stopped at farms to ask whether they could take any dead animals off the farmer's hands, and this no doubt perpetuates the impression of unhygienic eating habits, but this has in fact been a means of obtaining meat from householders who are glad not to have to bury a dead, and presumably infected, pig or calf. But in such cases the animals have already been killed deliberately and in secret by the same Romanies, who would have perhaps fed them an undetectable poison (*farmači*) or caused suffocation (*tasipe*), e.g. by feeding them a particular fast-growing mould which adheres to the mucous membrane in the throat.

Etiquette

Dishes tend to be stewed or fried, and should always be made available to a Romani guest. Not offering something to eat – and for that matter refusing to accept something offered – is a serious breach of etiquette, because it suggests that the person slighted in this way is not clean. Leaving a little on the plate also suggests that one's host has provided too much, and relieves him of being put in the position of having to offer more when he may not have enough to be able to do so. Helping oneself unbidden to food from someone else's plate is considered rude, but offering the best piece of meat from your own plate to someone else is certainly a good thing to do. If you are invited to sit at table when others are eating, you should eat something too; looking directly at someone who is eating when you aren't is not a good idea, since malicious thoughts can enter the body through the mouth with the food. It's better for you to be eating as well and if not, to say *te xas sastimasa* (or *te xan sastimasa* to more than one): 'may you eat in health'.

Indian parallels

While eating habits and the techniques of food preparation among the various populations throughout northern India have much in common, it is from Rajasthan and the Panjab that our people originated, and it is among the modern-day Banjara that persuasive historical parallels may be sought. Ideas of ritual pollution, so central to Romani belief, existed in the eleventh century caste system and continue to exist today; thus members of the same *jati* (sub-caste) may eat together without risk of contamination, for example, but will become polluted if they eat with members of other jatis; and because the jatis of one's associates might not always be known, contact between the mouth and the various utensils shared with others at a meal is avoided, just to be on the safe side. In conservative Romani culture, liquids are poured into the mouth from a container held away from the lips, so that the rim of the vessel (the *kerlo*) is not touched; smoke from a shared tobacco pipe is drawn (in the Romani language *pilo* or 'drunk', as in Hindi, rather than 'sucked' as in European languages) through the fist clenched around its stem, again to avoid making contact with the mouth. The surest way not to touch utensils used by others is to eat with the fingers, and every one of these habits is to be found among Romanies today.

Like the Rajputs, some of us divide foods into 'ordinary' and 'auspicious' or 'lucky' (*baxtalo)* categories (the Rajputs' terms for these two categories mean 'cold' and 'hot', though these have nothing to do with either temperature or pepper); this distinction reflects the close relationship between food and health, a particular ingredient being not only beneficial to the physical self but also to the spiritual. *Baxtale xajmata* or 'auspicious foods' include those which are pungent or strongly flavoured, such as garlic, lemon, pickles, peppers, sour cream and so on. The use of red pepper in some traditional Romani dishes is typical of Rajput cuisine particularly, and such food is called *ito* or 'piquant' (peppery) in Vlax Romani (from the Romanian word *iute*). Also in common with Indian culinary behaviour, is the practice of not preparing dishes far in advance of their being eaten, and of not keeping left over food. Dishes set for the dead at a *pomana* (wake) table or a *slava* (saint's day) table are eventually disposed of by being offered to passers-by, never just thrown away. Bread holds a very special place, and no meal is complete without it. It should never be thrown away; if it is, or if it is dropped, it might be apologised to. A hollowed-out cottage loaf is passed around at a wedding to collect donations of money for the bride and groom.

There are many customs associated with food and eating: potatoes (*kolompirja*) are not eaten at a pomana, nor can there be an even number of chairs at a pomana table; greens (*zelenimata*) are not eaten while one is in mourning, or expecting a baby, and so on. The origins of these practices are lost in time and may never be known; for many groups they have already been abandoned and forgotten, but for many others, they remain a part of the routine of life.

A few recipes

Some typical dishes, selected from a number of different Romani groups are listed here, those of them with * include directions for their preparation which you can follow:

Ankruste, are small baked cakes made from cornmeal, flavoured with coriander and cuminseed.

* ***Blini pherdile litjarde masesa*** are meat-filled crêpes. A *blina* is a very thin pancake and it is used to wrap the meat. In a bowl break two eggs, add a cup of milk, and a cup of flour, and beat to a thin batter. Pour half a cup of this into a frying pan containing a little melted butter, tilt the pan in a circular motion to coat the whole bottom with the batter and cook on both sides until you have a thin, circular yellow pancake, browned in spots, then set aside. You should have five or six of these. In another pan, mix together half a pound of very lean minced beef, a quarter pound of finely chopped ham, the trimmed and chopped white ends of ten spring onions, salt and black pepper to taste, a tablespoon of bacon fat, half a cup of sour cream, and a cup of

water. Cook until everything is soft and the water has evaporated. The mixture should be a coarse paste, and you should not be able to see the bits of ham or onion. If you can, add more water and cook longer. When it is cool, fashion a quantity of the meat into a squarish flattened ball in your hands and place in the middle of the blina. Fold the four sides of the blina over the meat, to make a small square, and press down gently. These are served with a sauce made as follows: take a pound of mushrooms and peel them, and chop them very fine. Cook them in melted butter. When they are cooked, add to the pot two finely chopped large tomatoes, preferably skinned. Season with salt, black pepper and red pepper. Continue to cook until the tomatoes have become soft, then add two thirds of a cup of sour cream and mix all of these ingredients together. This sauce is spooned hot over the blina. A spoonful of sour cream can be dolloped on top.

Bokoli or **pogača** is wheat bread made with baking soda but no yeast, sometimes with crumbled fried bacon stirred into the dough before baking.

Boranija is a meat and green-bean stew.

* **Cignidaki zumi** is a soup made with the leaves of the stinging nettle plant. Variations of this are found in Romani cuisines throughout Europe. Gather about a pound of nettles, the younger, lighter green leaves are best, and rinse several times. Separate the leaves from the stalks, which discard. Chop coarsely and boil in three pints of water with pork cut into small chunks, with or without small pieces of cut-up chicken added, total meat to make up a half pound before cooking. When almost done, thicken with flour and add half a cup of cooked mashed rhubarb. A spoonful of vinegar is added to most Romani stews, and may be added here.

Djeveli, an omelette made from the eggs of chickens or game birds.

Djuveči is a curry-like fish stew. The fish is partly cooked in a water-and-vinegar mixture before it is transferred to the stew; this prevents it from falling apart.

* **Galuški** are small dumplings made from flour and water, flavoured with almonds and boiled in milk. Mix a cup of flour, a teaspoonful of baking powder, a half a cup of ground almonds and a half a cup of sugar together, with enough water to make a stiff paste. You can use marzipan paste instead of ground almonds, in which case do not add any sugar. Fashion into small pellets as big as the end of your thumb,

and drop into boiling milk. Cook until they swell up and float to the top, and serve them in a bowl with the milk they were cooked in.

* ***Gembeci*** are dumplings made with flour and suet, stuffed with fried meat and cooked in a stew. Knead two cups of flour together with a cup of finely chopped beef suet or tallow (*khoni*) from which all the blood and tissue have been removed, and a tablespoonful of baking powder. Add a teaspoonful of chopped parsley and some salt and pepper to taste, and enough water to make a stiff paste that won't stick to your hands. In a pan, fry chopped up bacon or speck or ground pork, or a mixture of any of these, let cool, drain and set aside. Taking a lump of the dough (the *xumer*), press it into a thick flat circle in the palm of one hand, and put a generous spoonful of the fried meat into the middle. Fold the dough around it, sealing it over the top so that the meat is completely encased. Be careful not to let any oil run off while you're doing this, or the dough won't stick. Shape these into balls and drop them into whatever (thin) stew you're preparing, and they will swell up and cook together.

Gužvara is a kind of strudel made of cooked fruit folded or layered in pastry.

Hočiwiči or ***Niglo*** is hedgehog, especially favoured among Romanichals in France and Britain, but also eaten by other groups. There are different ways of preparing this animal, all involving cleaning and sometimes stuffing it, and various ways of removing its spines. One method is to encase the animal in clay and bake it, the spines coming off with the hardened clay once cooked; groups who find this method unclean might singe the spines off over a fire instead.

Jaxnija is a thick minced meat and red bean soup.

Manrro la smetanasa is a piece of bread spread with sour cream and stewed fruit.

Muterdo šax is the dandelion plant, its leaves are used as a green vegetable and its root may be dried, scorched and ground up to make a coffee-like drink.

Peržala is eggs scrambled with bits of fried meat or with herbs.

* ***Pirogo*** or ***pirogi*** is a dish made from noodles, cheese, currants and raisins. Boil until soft a pound of flat noodles in water flavored with honey and coloured with a little saffron, and drain. Spread a layer on the bottom of a well-buttered deep dish, and spread this with cream cheese. You will have to stir this to make it very soft, and dot it on, to

avoid moving the noodles; a beaten egg may optionally be added to this mixture. Sprinkle a layer of raisins and currants on the cream cheese, then place another layer of noodles on top of that and repeat. Do this as often as you want, making the top layer noodles, perhaps in some kind of decorative design. Dot with butter and bake in a hot oven until the top is brown and crispy. The raisins can be soaked in fruit juice or a fruit spirit such as slivovica or palenka before being used in the recipe.

Pirožna makoske semincjansa is a small cake filled with poppy-seed paste.

Poovengur drey a koori. A favourite with Romanichals, this is a potato, scrubbed and hollowed out, filled with jam and baked in a tin can with the lid tightly on, in the ashes.

Pufa or *Manriklo* is a flat yeast or (more often) soda raised bread cooked in a pan with oil, not unlike Native American 'frybread' or Indian *nan* in appearance.

Rrunza is a pig's stomach lining, cut into small pieces and stewed for several hours with peppers, tomatoes and onions, and flavored with salt, vinegar and lemon juice.

Rromano Čajo is 'Romani tea', drunk in a glass with peaches or straw-berries in it.

* *Sarmi* are cabbage leaves stuffed with a meat, rice and pepper mixture, cooked in tomato sauce. There are different ways to make a sarma. Here's one: take a large cabbage and remove a few of the outer leaves, being very careful not to tear them. Pare off some of the thick stalk to make this part of the leaf much thinner, and place into boiling water to soften. Set aside. In a bowl, mix a cup of fried minced beef, or fried minced ham, or both, and a cup of boiled white rice, salt and black pepper, and some chopped, cooked green peppers, such as jalapeño, to taste but the sarma should be *ito* (pepper-hot). Take some of this mixture, which should hold together in your hand, and wrap it in a cabbage leaf, to make a sealed rectangular package which you can fasten with thread or with a couple of toothpicks. Put the prepared sarmi in a shallow pan and cook them gently in seasoned tomato sauce for another 30-40 minutes.

Šonko fusujansa is a tomato-based casserole of ham chunks and butter beans.

Šutlo šax is a cabbage-based casserole made with chicken or pork, and
   seasoned with pepper and vinegar.
Xevica or **mamaliga** is porridge made from boiled cornmeal, the main
   staple of the Romanian slaves and still commonly eaten in that
   country.

Questions

1   Is there a common Romani cuisine? Why, or why not?
2   Say what you can about 'auspicious foods'.
3   Some Romanies kiss a piece of bread before eating it. Why
    do you think bread holds such significance for them?

CHAPTER TEN

Health

_____

B ecause access to physicians and hospitals is only sought in extreme cases due to their polluting association, and because Romanies have not generally been accommodated by them anyway, safeguarding the health of the community *within* the community is of special importance. Like the Rajputs, Vlax Romanies divide illnesses into two categories, those which are natural to the group, *rromane nasvalimata* – such things as heart complaints, rashes, vomiting, hiccups, insomnia or irritability – and those which are the result of over-familiarity with the *jado* or non-Romani world, *gadžikane nasvalimata*. These latter include, for example, all sexually transmitted diseases. For such afflictions, a non-Romani physician needs to be consulted; but for 'Romani afflictions', traditional cures are provided by a *drabarni* or female healer. This is the same as the Rajputs' *sīāna*. The root of the word *drabarni* is *drab* which means 'medicine' (from Sanskrit *dravya* "medication", compare the Hindi word *darb*). It is also the root of the verb *drabar-* which is usually translated in English as 'to tell fortunes', but which from the Romani perspective means 'making well'. When speaking English, Romanies prefer to call this skill brought from India 'advising' rather than 'fortune telling', for which another verb, *duriker-* exists.

If it is necessary for a person who has contracted a *gadžikano nas-valipe* to be admitted to hospital, relatives and others will go to him, often in considerable numbers, to provide *dji* and help restore balance. "Relatives, their relatives, and friends of a Gypsy flock around his hospital bed because [of] their culture" (Anderson and Tighe, 1973:282); only recently have hospital administrations begun to recognise this as cultural behaviour and to accommodate it (Salloway, 1973; Shields, 1981;

Thomas, 1985). Depending upon the nature of the non-Romani affliction, the individual may be declared defiled; not visited in hospital but instead banished from the community. This is invariably the response when this is e.g. syphilis, AIDS, or other such disease. Infections of this kind are a clear indication of a too-personal involvement in the non-Romani world, since it is assumed that they could never be contracted within the ethnic community.

As in all cultures, a clear link is understood to exist between diet and health; the fact that some foods are considered to be particularly 'auspicious', that is to say beneficial to our spiritual as well as our physical wellbeing, has already been mentioned. Some other edible plants are not used for food at all, but are entirely medicinal. These days, knowledge of traditional herbal medicine is being lost, because commercial medication is so easily available; but while we might buy aspirin today for a headache, not so long ago our grandparents would have taken the bark from a willow tree (called the *rukh rovindoj*) and boiled it into an extract for the same purpose; it only became known in recent times that willow bark in fact contains the same chemical as aspirin. In the same way, the leaves from a chestnut tree (*kastanengo rukh*) produce an extract for treating bronchitis, the vinca or periwinkle flower (*djiveski luludji*) a medicine for diabetes, the lily (*krina*) for various heart complaints, and the boiled-down petals of the rosemary plant (*loliorri*) make a rinse for dandruff.

Tradition aside, the real overall state of health in the Romani population is not good. Almost everywhere – in both eastern and western Europe and overseas – the life expectancy is generally lower than the national average, and the rate of infant mortality higher. There are a number of reasons for this; an unwillingness to visit physicians and clinics, the difficulty of getting to such facilities because of physical isolation or lack of transport, the often poor treatment provided to Romanies when they do manage to see a doctor, and the poor sanitary conditions and inadequate diet Romanies must live with daily in many places. Even in places where there is an abundance of food, health is still a concern. In the United States, for instance, the average life expectancy for a group of men studied was found to be forty-eight years (Thomas, et al., 1987:379). Diabetes and high cholesterol and blood pressure levels leading to heart attack were found in people younger than thirty. In some places where this is a problem, it is the result of inadequate nutrition; in others, it is because the traditional high fat diet is still maintained when modern daily life is no longer sufficiently vigorous to use up the calories. Sometimes, custom would seem to work against an adequate diet – expectant mothers in some groups cannot eat green vegetables, for example, at the time when they would be especially beneficial. Programs involving Romanies should make diet and health high priority areas of education.

Questions

1 Explain the concepts of Romani and non-Romani illnesses.
2 Why do Romanies visit sick relatives who are in hospital, in such large numbers? Should hospital authorities allow it?
3 Say what you can about 'traditional' medicine. Do you use any traditional remedies in your own home?

CHAPTER ELEVEN

How to interact with Romanies

T he first thing to remember when interacting with Romanies is that we are people just like you. When the slave owners said we didn't feel pain as much as you do, and that we could stand the cold much better than you do, and that we valued life less than you do, they were *wrong*. When cartoonists depict us as preferring to live in filth, they are *wrong*; we feel the same pain and joy and fear as you, we want the best for our children, and we want a comfortable home – just like you. Maybe these negative ideas about us arose because we learnt to keep our feelings to ourselves and not complain for fear of punishment. Maybe they came from a psychological desire on the part of the non-Romani world to make us somehow less that what *it* is, because then our feelings wouldn't matter so much and there would be less reason for guilt. But the 'gypsy' who is sweeping the street, or who comes into your home every day to look after your children, or who sits outside the train station asking for money has a life too, though one quite separate from yours; maybe he or she has children at home, who desperately miss mama or tata; maybe he or she has an elderly relative who needs constant attention but who isn't getting it. Maybe he or she doesn't know where a warm, safe place to sleep will be found during the cold night ahead, or where the next meal will come from. But maybe too, a Romani you meet has a nice home, with a loving and respectful family, and is looking forward to enjoying dinner with them later in the day. Maybe he or she has a university degree, or is a successful artist; you just don't know, and it is a mistake to jump to conclusions before you do.

Try to change places, in your mind, with the Romani person you are dealing with. Is it a child in your school? Suppose that you are she. Can she speak Slovak, or Bulgarian, or Romanian as well as the other children in the class? Has she already been pushed aside, and placed in a special class for 'disadvantaged' or 'backward' children? If so, they will mostly be other Romanies like herself, since over 50 per cent of all Romani schoolchildren in some countries – are placed in special classes which effectively guarantee that they will never have a place in the mainstream of society. Would you want that for your own child?

Attitudes must be examined. Not speaking the national language fluently may be a problem, but it is one that can be solved. It is dealt with quite successfully in countries where there are bilingual programs in the schools, and where teacher training includes courses in bilingual and bicultural education. And think about this – a Romani child may not have complete fluency in the national language, but can certainly speak it, and is therefore bilingual. How many non-Romani classmates are bilingual? This is surely a positive skill, and should be acknowledged as such.

If Romani children don't always do well on tests, it may be because the world they come from is very different from your own, with different heroes and different villains, with different values placed on such fundamental concepts as how husbands and wives, mothers and fathers, and even domestic pets fit into their universe. Someone who may be presented in class as a nationally-revered historical figure for you non-Romanies could well be the same person who once sent our people to their deaths, or had Romani families broken apart and imprisoned or shipped overseas. If tests are constructed around the norms of the majority culture, those not a part of it cannot hope to do as well as those for whom it reflects a familiar world. How successfully would non-Romani children fare, if they had to pass a test devised from the Romani perspective?

Your immediate reaction may be "but they are citizens of this country, and must know the language and culture of this country". And it is perfectly understandable that you would think that. But while those things come naturally to non-Romani children when they are growing up, Romani youngsters don't have that background, and must 'catch up'. Experience in other multi-ethnic countries has shown very clearly that recognising and respecting the languages and cultures of minority populations strengthens national pride and is good for the whole country. A government which encourages members of its ethnic minorities to be proud of who they are is a government that will make those same people proud to live in such a country. The worst thing a country can have is a large section of its population feeling left out and unhappy; the consequences of this are well known in history.

You might ask "why should those people receive special treatment?" and perhaps you feel resentful or angry or even threatened because you think they're getting it. But is acknowledgment of a people's cultural and linguistic differences really 'special treatment'? Isn't that already there for members of the majority population? National minorities outside of their homelands – ethnic Hungarians in Romania or Slovakia, for example, or Russians in Lithuania – want to maintain their languages and customs and have their own schools and churches, and so they should, while at the same time participating fully in the larger society. We want nothing different from what is wanted by other groups in Europe. Polls conducted among European Romanies during the 1990s show that most would like to be integrated – though not necessarily assimilated – into non-Romani society. Some more conservative Romani populations, a small minority living mostly in eastern Europe, however, do not. Like orthodox Muslims or Jews or Hindus, 'orthodox' Romanies wish to remain quite separate. Those people should be accommodated in the same way as those other groups, but they are not the people you are likely to be interacting with in your daily life.

Try to get to know your Romani acquaintances or pupils. Don't expect immediate warmth or trust, it hasn't been generally forthcoming from you non-Romanies in the past, and there is little reason for us to think that everything has suddenly changed overnight. Learn more about real Romani history. Don't assume that every Romani is an expert and can answer all your questions, and be *very* careful of what you read. Even 'serious' works may only strengthen negative stereotypes. For example, a one-time leading specialist on Romanies in Hungary, József Vekerdi, wrote (1988:14) that:

> The Gypsies' ancestors began leaving northwest India probably about the seventh century AD. They are characterized as robbers, murderers, hangmen and entertainers. These professions were prescribed for them by the rulers of the Hindu caste system. Thus they belonged to the so-called 'wandering criminal tribes' of India and were obliged to lead a parasitic way of life. Among the numerous outcast groups, they occupied the lowest rung on the social scale.

Not only is the time of the exodus too early by nearly four centuries, but the identity of the pre-Romani population is merely a guess based on biased preconceptions, and his classification *wandering criminal tribes* is taken from colonial terminology that dates only from the late nineteenth century during the British occupation of that country. The details of our history outlined in the present book, tell a very different story.

There are many misleading stereotypes that have to be replaced with facts, and which must be challenged and understood: the belief that we steal, that we are dirty, that we can't stay in one place, that we have no morals, and that we practice magical arts and place curses on people. Each of these is examined here:

Crime

Certainly some of us break the law. So do some of you. Yet an examination of the percentage of our people in prison would lead anyone to think that we really were a "whole race of criminals" as the professor of criminology, Cesare Lombroso, once called us. After all, if we are only, say, 15 per cent of the population, and yet make up 80 per cent of the people in jail in some countries, this must prove something: surely the facts don't lie. Hitler believed that 'criminality' was an inherited, genetic disease characterizing our people, and this was his reason for trying to exterminate us. But when we look at the 'crimes' listed in Dillmann's *Zigeuner-Buch*, they are such things as trespassing, lighting campfires, poaching, or grazing horses on private property, stealing fruit and vegetables from farms and orchards and so on. When we examine the crimes for which we are arrested today, they are usually theft, sometimes public nuisance, sometimes trespassing. Hardly ever embezzlement, or murder, or rape, or extortion, which are much more highly represented offences among non-Romanies.

In the past, when laws existed which prevented Romanies from stopping in a place or entering a town, trespassing was a frequent occurrence. Sometimes it was done unwittingly, because of our not being able to read posted signs – which is why so many such warnings took the form of pictures instead. Even today, there are many shopkeepers and café owners who refuse to serve us. Our babies need feeding too – anyone who was desperate enough would take food if they were continually denied service in shops and restaurants.

The idea that we steal babies has been a theme in novels and films, and has even been the subject of a masters thesis (Meyers, 1987; see also Shields, 1993). There is no evidence for this; it is difficult enough providing for our own children. On the other hand, it has traditionally been seen as a very great disgrace for an unmarried girl to find herself expecting a baby, and there are cases on record of such young non-Romani women leaving their infants with Romanies to care for. 'Running away with the gypsies' voluntarily is also a fantasy which finds its way into literature, and which can easily be reinterpreted as being 'stolen by gypsies'. An editorial in an Australian paper (Norton, 1927:1) warned readers of the likelihood of their children being kidnapped:

For centuries, the wandering Gypsy folk have frightened parents all over the world … adult Gypsies should not, on any account, be allowed to associate with white children in such a restricted area as a schoolroom or a playground. The confined spaces lend themselves too well to eventualities that might well cause fear [of their being kidnapped] in the heart of any parent.

"Gypsies Steal Children!"

Most Romani 'crime' in fact consists of petty offences; why then such over-representation in the jails? Studies show that what is now called 'profiling' is very common where Romanies are concerned. This means stopping and questioning a person just because he is what is sometimes called a 'visible minority', identifiable by his physical appearance. Police will apprehend Romanies just because they are Romanies and for no other reason, and are more ready to find charges to file against them. In the courtroom too, sentencing for the same crime or misdemeanour is

Two posters, one British and one French, both depicting the supposed Romani penchant for using knives to settle matters.

very often harsher for us than for you. One example from the United States illustrates this very well: in 1990 the newspapers reported a Romani woman and her daughter who were convicted of cheating a client out of several thousand dollars in a fortune-telling scheme, and who between them received a sentence of over two hundred years in prison in New York. In the same week those same newspapers also ran a story about a (non-Romani) television evangelist in Atlanta who had cheated the public out of several *million* dollars in the name of religion, but who received just a few years in jail. He is now a free person once again (Hancock, 1992:7–8). There is a long tradition of this kind of double standard; the Moldavian Civil Code in the seventeenth century included two laws, one stating that the *Ţigan* (Romani slave) who violated a woman would be burnt alive, but a Romanian guilty of the same charge "shall not be punished at all". It is important too, to compare the nature and extent of wrongdoing in order to keep a balanced perspective. Thomas Acton (quoted in Hancock, 1992:7) wrote that:

Compared with the massive record of murder, theft, kidnapping and other crimes by non-Gypsies against Gypsies throughout history, Gypsy crime against non-Gypsies pales almost into insignificance, so that to prioretize the study of the latter over the former shows a twisted sense of values.

None of this excuses law breaking on the part of Romanies. It merely explains it. It is not exclusive to our people, and is a legacy from a time when it was one mechanism for subsistence and survival. But it shouldn't have to be necessary any more. Romani lawbreakers should be subject to exactly the same laws and penalties as anyone else in society, and not be treated differently because of their ethnicity. To do so is discrimination, which is wrong, both morally and legally. Those guilty of racism and dis-crimination should likewise have to pay the penalty. Keep in mind too that crime is not an ethnic problem, but a social one, and *any* group that is socially excluded from enjoying all the benefits of a society is more likely to resort to crime than one that does.

Slave mentality

Some Romanies bear another, heavier legacy – a perspective on life inherited from the hundreds of years of slavery. If, for centuries, a people have lived in a society where every single thing, including food, clothing and even one's spouse is provided from outside, i.e. at the discretion of the slave owner, and if getting anything extra, including favours, depends upon one's influence with that owner, then it will instill an assumption that this is how one survives in the world. And while slavery has been abolished now for a century and a half, remnants of this way of thinking are still in evidence. Not only are assistance and material things sought from outside rather than from within the community, but cultivating useful and influential contacts outside of the non-Romani world is also a priority, and becomes a mark of prestige within it. A man can become the leader of his community on that basis alone. This kind of thinking does not encourage self-determination or personal initiative; but before it can be addressed and changed, it has to be understood.

Anger

Given our image as carefree, happy-go-lucky Gypsies it comes as a sur-prise to some that there is a great deal of suppressed anger in our people.

"Why should we move?
That looks like a nice spot!"

Romanies are bitter and angry at the indignities that racism brings; angry at the advantages your children seem to have in their schooling and expectations from life. There is anger at the *gadžo* academics who have obtained their higher education as a matter of course and who are now making their professional reputations by studying us and our language. There is anger at the things the *gadžo* experts have written about us in their books and articles for all to see: that we are "liars ... parasites, boastful, arrogant and superstitious" as the 1911 edition of the *Encyclopedia Britannica* says, or that "the mental age of an average adult Gypsy" is "about that of a child of ten" as it says in its 1956 edition. As more of us become educated, the more we are learning about what has been said about us and what has been done to us. An elderly Kalderash man in Wichita broke down in tears of disbelief when his son told him that he had recently learnt that the Kalderasha had been slaves for hundreds of years. Beginning with Grellmann, our being compared with children as the *Britannica* did has become almost routine; Unn Jørstad, who was director of education for Romanies in Oslo in the 1970s concluded one report with the words "all of them are just like children" (1972:137). This paternalistic impression perhaps stems from the fact that Romanies haven't typically become involved in non-Romani affairs, or have wanted (or been offered) positions of authority within them. As a rule we are non-confrontational, and will go along with suggestions either for the sake of peace, or from a fear of challenging them. If

"Why move? This is a nice spot.

involvement of any kind becomes uncomfortable, the Romani response is to leave.

The long-term effects of discrimination are destructive. Madhu Kishwar (1998:14) has written about this:

> When people are constantly subject to humiliation and unmerited attack, they lose their sense of self-respect and often even start transforming their behaviour into that of the stereotyped image projected on them ... We would do well to remember, a people without self-respect do become dangerous – both to themselves and to others.

Suppressed anger and frustration may manifest themselves in different ways – in one's personal life as family violence and alcoholism, and outwardly as well. Billy Cribb, a Romani boxer from the south of England writes of how he was drawn towards this profession, so common among Romanies, when as a child he was made to feel different at school by the other children, and when his "only answer would be to hit them ... I couldn't answer in any other way" (Cribb, 2001:24). A similar account is found in Stockin (2000). Spanish Romanies say that the stamping feet, flashing eyes and violent gestures that are part of flamenco dance are a silent 'stylized aggression', an outlet which in the past reflected the resentment felt at being offered protection from racism by wealthy *patrones* but having to pay for it in return by entertaining them.

The cover of a novel about Romanies during the Second World War.

Personal hygiene

The idea that we are dirty is widespread. As explained in Chapter 7, a distinction is made between being physically dirty and being spiritually dirty, and under the best of conditions, the two states support each other. But for some Romanies who live in ghettos or *mahalas* where there is no plumbing or sanitation, and where many families must share a single well or pump and communal toilet, it is very difficult to maintain the standards everybody would like to have. The cartoons shown here depict Romanies choosing to live surrounded by garbage. Sometimes, when laws move families on, rubbish-dumps on the outskirts of town are one of the very few places where they can pull in with less chance of being moved on by the police. Sometimes, families who make a living dealing in scrap metal will find brass, copper and chrome in such places to collect and sell, and so will stop near them for that reason. Given equal access to the normal amenities, we are a people who are fastidious about personal cleanliness and hygiene. The time spent in the concentration camps during the *Porrajmos* was unbearable for our people, as it is today in refugee centres, where little or no provision is made for maintaining strict hygiene or for preparing food in a ritually clean way. Time spent in prison, too, is regarded with horror for the same reasons.

Nomadism

Travelling is a part of our history. Our ancestors trekked for thousands of miles from India to Europe and out into the world, so there is certainly some truth to the stereotype of the 'travelling gypsy'. But a distinction must be made between travelling on a journey, with a purpose, and travelling because local laws in an area forbid one to stop and therefore leave no choice.

Once reaching Europe, our ancestors soon became subject to legislation (especially in northern and western Europe) that kept them on the move. That being the case, ways of making a living had to be developed which were portable and which did not require fixed, heavy equipment. In time, occupations such as horse trading, metal-smithing, fortune telling and so on became family professions and have been kept up even when forced removal is no longer everywhere a factor. Remember that there is no 'genetic' disposition to travel; it is solely the result of circumstances.

The cover of Erich von Stroheim's novel *Paprika the Gypsy Trollop.*

Morals

There is a well-established pattern in western literature of representing non-western women as immodest and loose-moralled, and non-western men as a sexual threat to western women. This is even found in presentations meant for children; compare, for example, Walt Disney's depictions of Pocahontas (a Native American) or Esmerelda (a Romani) with his Cinderella or Snow White. Consider D H Lawrence's treatment of the 'gypsy man' in his novel *The Virgin and the Gypsy*. The basis for this

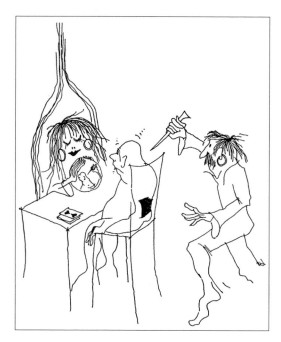

This cartoon from Germany combines all three stereotypes of stealing, fortune telling and knife-wielding.

may be the natural attraction of the 'exotic' or unattainable, but it may also be a way of underscoring, subconsciously, the perceived lesser value of non-western peoples. One writer describing a nineteenth century Romani encampment in Romania which he never actually visited, basing his account instead the writings of Grellmann and others (St. John, 1853:142), also edited in some opinions of his own:

Nothing can be more abominably filthy than the habits of this degraded tribe ... we are sorry to be obliged to add that both men and women are, as a rule, exceedingly debauched,

but this did not stop St. John from adding that "these bold, brown, beautiful women only make one astonished to think how such eyes, teeth and figures can exist in the stifling atmosphere of their tents" (*loc. cit.*). At the time and place he was describing, the Romani men known as the *scopiţi*, who drove the coaches and horses for the ladies of the aristocracy, were castrated by their owners because of the threat they were imagined to pose to their passengers. Félix Colson, the French diarist who visited a slaveholding estate in Wallachia in the 1830s, wrote of the female Romani slaves' being provided to guests as sexual entertainment, while at the same time being called "whores" by their owners (Colson, 1839:35).

Romani morals are in fact excessively strict by non-Romani standards; showing the legs, for example, is *gadžikani forma*, or non-Romani behaviour, and neither men nor women should wear shorts. The dancers who lift their colourful skirts on the stage of the *Teatr Romen* are all non-Romanies, since the Romani members of the troupe will not do this. Virginity at the time of a first marriage is required and discovery of its

A cartoon strip from the British comic *Viz*, 1990.

absence are grounds enough for the marriage to be terminated. Topics concerning sex or other bodily functions are strenuously avoided in mixed company. When the issue of body searches came up in a court case in the United States involving the illegal entry by the police into a Romani household, all of the Romani women in the courtroom arose and left; simply to be in mixed company when this was being discussed was improper. It is not at all polite to talk about visiting the lavatory, or whether a woman is expecting a baby, or, in some groups, to talk about going to bed or even to say that word. If there are Romani girls and women who are prostitutes today, you can imagine how desperate their families' situations must be to allow this.

Magic

The image of a 'gypsy with a crystal ball' or tarot cards is very common, and there are many books on Romani magic, fortune-telling and curses. Fortune-telling is a widespread means of income, for reasons that are easily understood: it is a tradition brought from India, it requires little or no equipment and can be done anywhere, there is a steady demand from the non-Romani public to have predictions made about the future, and it is a skill which gives Romanies a small measure of control and protection. It should also be kept in mind that not all groups practice fortune-telling, for instance the Bashalde – the Hungarian-Slovak Romanies in the United States – who emphatically state that this is something which distinguishes them from the *Laxe* (the Kalderash). And consider for one moment – if we really had magical powers, why haven't we used them to improve our own situation? To bring an end to antigypsyism, and to acquire wealth?

Our stereotypes of non-Romanies

It surprises some people to learn that just as you have stereotypes of 'gypsies', we have stereotypes of you non-Romanies as well. It is commonly believed, for example, that non-Romani men and women are insecure about what behaviour is appropriate for their respective genders: should a man cry, or cook? Should a woman swear, or wear trousers? Non-Romanies are thought not to have respect for age, putting their aging parents into homes, and allowing the children to speak rudely to their elders. It is believed by some that non-Romanies will happily talk about the most intimate details of their private lives to complete strangers; that they announce the fact to everyone that they need to visit the toilet and then don't wash their hands afterwards. That they allow their pets to sleep on their beds and to eat from the same plates that they use themselves; that their young women are immodest in their dress and sexual behaviour.

These, of course, are stereotypes, and they are surprisingly like your own notions about us. They are no more typical of your non-Romani behaviour than your ideas about Romanies are typical of us, and while some of them may describe some people, no single person has all of them and some individuals have none of them at all. Once we become individual people to each other, we stop being representatives of an entire group, labeled with all of the stereotypes associated with that group. There is a saying in our language, that *kana jekh Rrom si došalo, sa'l Rrom si došale*, "when one Romani is guilty, all Romanies are guilty". It shouldn't have to be that way.

Some suggestions

When you talk to us, be sincere, and say what you want; we have a lot of practice in recognising insincerity. When non-Romanies have come asking questions it usually has not been to benefit us, but just the contrary. Eva Justin, who worked with Robert Ritter in the Race Hygiene

Centre in Germany collecting genealogical data on who had 'Gypsy blood' pretended to be our friend, asking for the names of relatives so that she could warn them of what was in store. She was even given a pet name, *Loli Tschai*, because of her red hair. But she was turning all of the information she collected over to the Nazis to make it easier for them to find us. Sometimes people befriend Romanies because they are writing a book or a dissertation, but they won't tell us that. Don't 'collect' us as curios in an insincere way and then abandon us, but be straightforward, don't be shy to express your curiosity or your desire simply to be a friend. And if you meet with skepticism or suspicion at first on our part, be patient. Many real friendships have eventually been made in this way.

Above all, remember that we are people, with names that our parents gave us. When a Romani character turns up in a novel he usually has no name, simply being identified as 'the gypsy'. Call us by our personal names, so that we are identified as individuals; don't refer to the child in your class or your waiting room as 'the gypsy'. This should also be the rule in newspaper accounts; unless the ethnicity of a person being written about is essential to the story, don't include it gratuitously. And don't be tempted to provide other clues just for the sake of it, such as "the dark-skinned Mr Lakatosz" or "Mrs Cooper who lives on a trailer site" unless they add constructively to your report. And speaking of names, don't decide what we as a people are to be called. A certain European government wanted to make the horribly offensive word *Tsigan* our official designation; one writer argued that *Gypsy* was perfectly acceptable because it is what Romanies in Hungary, Germany and elsewhere call themselves. Of course they don't – *Gypsy* is an English word. Someone once said that those who are in control of a people's name are in control of those people themselves.

If you're writing about Romanies, avoid such words as 'wander' and 'roam', since they suggest aimlessness and lack of purpose, and perhaps the luxury simply to travel at one's whim. Don't say that we live in 'tribes' – that word should only be used in its proper sociological sense, and generally speaking, Romani social structure isn't tribal. Don't speak of the 'gypsy lifestyle', but refer instead to 'the Romani way of life'. Our culture is not 'stylish', except as it is perceived to be in fashion magazines; it is rooted in a tradition a thousand years old. And besides, we are not one monolithic whole; there are many Romani 'ways of life'. Most of what is in this book, for example, only describes the language

A cartoon from the magazine *Buhazi* reflecting a common Romani attitude towards the non-Romani 'experts'.

and customs of Vlax Romanies, and it would be a mistake to think that it applies to all groups everywhere.

Don't let your choice of words add to the 'strange' image of Romanies when you write about us; one journalist wrote of our origins as being "shrouded in mystery" (Godwin, 2001:78), when he could just as easily have said that they were not known at the time that he was referring to. If such wording would not be used when describing other populations, it serves no purpose to use it to describe Romanies; a description of New Zealanders wouldn't say that they "were thought to descend from British immigrants", yet Kingfisher Publication's *Children's Encyclopedia* (New York, 1994:318) still writes that "Gypsies … probably came from India" and the 2002 edition of *Pears Cyclopedia*, like so many other encyclopedias has at its entry for *Gypsies* "a nomadic race, *believed to be* of Indian origin" (Cook, 2002:L54, emphasis added). The Cowan Report mentioned in Chapter 1 says of this "the Roma are genetically closer to Asians than to surrounding Europeans. This conclusion can hardly be described as exciting news; it has taken genetics 70 years and several thousand blood samples to confirm what has been known to linguists for the past 200 years" (Kalaydjieva et al., 1999:13).

Don't make uninformed statements about us, such as "Romanies have no religion" or "Romanies don't have a written language" or "Romanies are afraid of water" or "Romanies never lie to other Romanies"; better to ask us directly than to repeat this kind of misinformation taken from books and assume automatically that what you've read about us is true. The older written sources are usually full of mistakes. In one book, Manfri Woods' *In the Life of a Romany Gypsy* (1973), a whole creation myth and religion was invented, and has been repeated as fact in at least four other published works since then. Some recommended titles of

sources which are reliable are provided in Chapter 15.

For a lot of people, the first and only Romani person they've ever met comes to represent *all* Romanies for them. Each one of us is different – don't judge an entire people on just one individual. Similarly, students newly come to Romani Studies may judge all subsequently-encountered groups by the first that they got to know – a characteristic that one writer has called "Kalderashocentrism". There are great differences among Romani groups, and what might appear to be 'more Romani' in one rather than another may turn out simply to be a custom adopted from the local non-Romani population.

The idea of having some "Gypsy blood" is an attractive one to some non-Romanies; a cartoon from the short-lived newsletter *Dukhum*.

Don't imply that our way of life is archaic by asking whether we 'still' do things ("do they still arrange their marriages?") – this is another way of suggesting that we 'still' have a way to go before we catch up with you. And at the same time, don't be disappointed when we don't match the Hollywood small-*g* gypsy image. One journalist, writing an article about Romanies for an American newspaper included the words "sadly, some of them are now living in houses". If that writer had actually met any of us, he'd have known that fewer than three per cent of Romani Americans live permanently in trailers today. When non-Romanies abandon their older customs, they call it 'progress', but if *we* do, we're seen as losing our 'gypsiness'. Don't try to save us from that, or show us how to be more 'gypsy' the way the English woman "Indian Kathy" tried to do and who,

Another *Buhazi* cartoon.

dressed in bead-and-feather adorned buckskins, rides her piebald stallion Indian-style along the roads of Kent. She is seeking out gypsies in their roadside camps to restore their pride and their forgotten crafts (Zygmant, 1974:16).

It isn't necessary to try to become one of us by giving yourself a Romani name, or dressing in 'gypsy-like' fashion, or calling us 'brother' and 'sister'. At the same time, conforming sensibly in some ways where dress is concerned will certainly help you and us both feel comfortable together, particularly regarding how you clothe your lower body. The appeal of having some 'Gypsy blood' is not uncommon among non-Romanies, but if such a wish were ever realised, it might not prove to be so romantic. To paraphrase Arigon Starr, "everyone wants to be a Gypsy, but if they could, they'd find it scary. You're in a place where you're invisible" (Elkind, 2000:1).

We are both *here* and *now*, so please address us as 'you' and not 'they' when you are talking directly to us – by calling us 'they' you are removing us to another place away from you and not acknowledging who is right there in front of you. And when writing about us, don't describe our way of life in the past tense – by doing that, you are removing us to another time. An example of this distancing us from the present, as well as of grossly distorting our culture, is found in one encyclopedia (Walker, 1983:361):

> The matriarch was the center of gypsy tribal life. Everything that went on around a tribal mother resembled the old pagan sex rites. Her husband was a drone, whose function was to impregnate her. The tribe supported him in idleness, but looked down on him as a non-productive member if he failed to beget perfect children.

Sometimes in the portrayal of our people, and in films especially, characteristics typical of quite distinct Romani groups are all thrown together, so that in a scene which takes place in Ukraine or Lithuania, for example, the actors might be shown wearing Spanish Romani clothes and living in British Romani waggons. In novels, when the author wishes to include some of our language for authenticity, British Romanichal Romani words (usually traceable to the writings of George Borrow) are put in the mouths of Hungarian or Russian Romanies, or else British Romanichals will be described as participating in a *kris*, the internal legal system specific to Vlax Romanies. This kind of misrepresentation is relatively harmless, except that it helps keep alive an inaccurate idea of what we are really like.

In more serious situations of conflict or misunderstanding, the best solution is very often compromise – neither side being 100 per cent satisfied, but attempting to work together by meeting half way. Sitting down and talking, getting to know each other as equals, is the first step to starting this process. And who knows – when you get to know us better, you might discover fascinating aspects of the Romani world that you never dreamt existed.

You can be a very real factor in the future peace and stability of your country. The Romani population is huge, numbering in the millions in Europe alone, and like the rest of the European population, it continues to grow. In May 2001 the British magazine *The Economist* reported that "In Slovakia, Gypsies ... might even become a majority in the country by 2060" (Ledgard, 2001:29). None of us is going anywhere, and we really have only one choice: to learn to live together. The alternatives are simply too awful to contemplate. Destroying whole populations, as the Nazis attempted to do, ultimately fail, but at tremendous cost. Maintaining a racially segregated society is miserable for everybody, and enormously expensive. Learning not just to tolerate each other but to respect each other as well is our only real option.

Suggestions like these have been made elsewhere. In August 1983, a Romani woman from Finland, Saga Weckman, attended the Eleventh International Congress of Anthropological and Ethnological Sciences in Quebec, and circulated a document there entitled *Researching Gypsies: Advice from a Romni*. Her comments are valuable because they come from a Romani person. They are given here:

1   Make yourself familiar with the essential elements of Romani culture and social organisation, no matter what is the actual research problem you are interested in.
2   When researching, be genuinely yourself. Do not try to 'become a Gypsy'. You can't. And do not try to over-please us.
3   Do not pigeonhole us into the framework of the governing majority and its science. It has been attempted for over 400 years already, with

little success. In some ways we are like other people, but hasty general-izations are dangerous.

4   Remember that you are the novice in Gypsy culture, not the expert. That is so, no matter how many degrees you have.

5   As is the case with any research into a culture, there is a common thread running through Romani culture. Without discovering that, any research on Gypsies will fail. Remember that you are dealing with a non-Euro-pean (or Euro-American) culture. Do not force us into a European mould. We are an eastern culture, as we come from India.

6   Never be satisfied with the first answer you get to a question.

7   Although we speak the *gadjikano* language besides our own, it may differ sometimes from that of the majority. That is not because our use of the language is inferior to yours, but it is different, with different meanings attached to the same words. Pay attention to meanings, not to words, to avoid misunderstandings. You might also be made fun of through the use of that same language.

8   Do not draw too-hasty conclusions, as they are usually the wrong ones.

9   Come 'down' to 'our level' from your pedestal. From a platform you can never reach us.

10   Try to leave your attitudes and prejudices outside the door. Do not compare us with yourself.

11   Be a humane human being.

12   Always use our expertise about ourselves, but use it – and us – correctly.

13   Gypsies love authenticity in all its forms. Be genuine when you are working with us.

14   Never betray the trust shown to you.

Since then, two more sets of such guidelines have appeared: one a small book from the Union Romani in Spain in 1998, prepared in cooperation with the European Commission and entitled *The Gipsy People: A Guide for Journalists* (available from *http://www.unionromani.org*), and the other a pamphlet published in Britain in 2000 by The Commission for Racial Equality, entitled *Travellers, Gypsies and the Media: Guidance to Journalists*, which is reproduced here:

- Poor quality reporting which exploits or panders to stereotypes can cause much hurt to those about whom the stories are written. By repeating false and negative stereotypes, the media can encourage bad practice on the part of those with whom Travellers and Gypsies deal and can validate the expression of language and attitudes which in any other circumstances would be seen as totally unacceptable.

- The Commission for Racial Equality has handled cases under the Race Relations Act for Travellers and Gypsies for over 20 years. The number of such cases continues to run at several dozen each year. The majority of these cases involve clear breaches of the Act. These guidelines are not intended to make the Media shy away from covering issues and stories to do with Travellers and Gypsies. Quite the contrary. The Commission for Racial Equality and those organisations representing Travellers and Gypsies want to see more coverage in the media but are keen to help the media develop a coverage that is honest and fair, open and inclusive.

- Steer clear of exploiting prejudice: the public wants a media that is campaigning, but those campaigns should be built on matters of genuine public concern, not simply prejudices against particular groups.
- Check the facts: go to the experts who can help to set the context. With these recommendations we include a list of contacts of individuals and organisations which can help you with various aspects of your story. Make sure that wherever possible you check the details with a relevant source, and don't just rely on expressions of local or popular prejudice. Many allegations are made about Travellers, Gypsies and now Roma asylum seekers from Eastern Europe, but can those making the allegations actually substantiate them?
- Don't let your news agenda only be driven by the way others are handling the issue: certain story-lines easily dominate media discussions of Travellers or Gypsies while issues of great importance to the communities involved are downplayed or ignored altogether. Don't write about Travellers or Gypsies only in the context of disputes over stopping places, look also at the problems they face.
- Look behind the story line: don't assume there is only one point of view. Always seek the views of Traveller and Gypsy organisations to see whether or not there is an alternative interpretation or a different and more significant story line to be presented.
- Listen to the people you are writing about: this is particularly important when it comes to the terms and language you use. Terms such as 'tinker', 'itinerant', or 'gyppo' are all highly offensive to those about whom they are used and should be avoided. The terms Traveller(s), Gypsy or Irish Traveller should be used with initial capital letters. Offensive stereotypes (for example 'scroungers', 'dole dodgers', 'bogus asylum seekers') should only be used when they are accurate descriptions of particular individuals, and should not be employed to negatively stereotype whole groups.
- Don't label people if it is not relevant. Reference to the fact that an individual is a Traveller, Gypsy or Irish Traveller should only be made when it is relevant and appropriate.

Questions

1 Do you have any Romani friends? If you do, how did your friendship begin? Have you eaten a meal in each other's home?
2 Should all the citizens of a country be as alike as possible? Can you think of a country which is like that?
3 What is the difference between *integration* and *assimilation*?
4 Have you ever had a bad personal experience with a Romani? Have you also had the same kind of experience with a non-Romani person? How did the two situations differ?
5 What is 'profiling'?
6 What is 'slave mentality'?
7 Where do the stereotypes of 'work-shy, carefree gypsies' and 'stealing babies' come from?
8 Say what you can about *fortune-telling* as a Romani occupation.
9 What do you think about the Romani stereotypes of non-Romanies? Do they make you angry?

CHAPTER TWELVE

The emergence of Romani organizations

Ekh dženo samas kana reslam k'a Oropate, thaj sam t'avas pale jekh dženo ("we were one people when we came into Europe, and we must be one people again").

Nationalist slogan

There have been Romani spokesmen for our people from the very beginning who have interacted with the non-Romani establishment and who have translated such Romani words as *Baro, Xulaj, Šerengro* as 'King', 'Earl', 'Duke' and so on. 'Gypsy Kings and Queens' still make good copy for pop journalists, although Romani society is not monarchical, and the equivalents of those words (*thagar, thagarni, amperato*, etc.) never occur as self-designations within *Rromanipen*. However, the activities of single individuals speaking for their group must be seen differently from large-scale efforts to reunite Romani populations that have become distinct from each other. It is widely felt that the fragmentation of our once cohesive population has been the result of hostile, external factors, not voluntary internal ones. After all, our ancestors made the journey from India to Europe intact.

There are probably many instances of Romani organisations having been formed but which have passed unrecorded into history. Bercovici wrote of a huge meeting in Switzerland of Romanies from all over Europe at the end of the fifteenth century; in 1722 a thousand armed Romanies united to fight (unsuccessfully) for their freedom from oppression in the German states. On 27 January 1872 the *London Times* published a brief notice about a conference of German Romanies that had taken place the year before in Darmstadt. This was a conference reported from Cannstadt, not Darmstadt, but which in fact never happened; it was

Gheorghe Nicolescu with some of his followers in Romania, 1930s.

invented by a journalist who wrote about it in the *Stuttgartner Zeitung* as a joke in the context of the annual Wurtemburg Festival, perhaps an indication of the lack of seriousness with which Romani affairs were viewed. A more accurately documented pan-European Romani conference took place seven years later at Kisfalu, in Hungary, in 1879. In the summer of 1905 a meeting of Romani leaders in Bulgaria convened in Sofia, among other things to press the government to allow Romanies to vote. On 1 June 1906 the *caribaši* of the Bulgarian Romanies, a man named Ramadan Ali, brought together Romani leaders from all over the country and drew up a petition demanding equal rights for his people, which he sent to the National Parliament. It was not acted upon, however. Stimulated by events in Europe, an application was filed in Washington in the United States two years later by members of the Serbian Romani Adams (Adamović) family, for the establishment of The National Gypsy Association of America. Its principal aims were to improve housing and education for American Romanies. Two decades later the Russian American Romani Steve Kaslov, founder of The Red Dress Gypsies' Association, approached President Roosevelt voicing the same concerns.

The *Near East Magazine* for 12 June 1913 reported that "a vast concourse of Gypsies" had gathered at Piatra Neamţ in Romania to pay tribute at the unveiling of a statue of Mihail Kogălniceanu, a nineteenth century journalist whose writings were influential in bringing an end to Romani slavery in his country (Chapter 2). The seeds of reunification, however, had been sown at the Kisfalu meeting some years before, and following the end of the First World War Romani political activity flourished in eastern Europe, particularly in Poland, Russia, Yugoslavia and Romania. In Russia, Romani activism was suppressed by Joseph Stalin, although until that date, The Pan-Russian Romani Union, under the leadership of Aleksander Germanov, had been increasingly successful in coordinating some thirty Romani-run artisan cooperatives in Moscow, and fifty collective estates throughout the western Soviet Union. The largest of these, home to seventy families, was established in Krikunovo in Caucasia, and bred horses for the Red Army. In Romania, The Association of Roma was founded at Clabour in 1926, and between 1930 and 1934 published a journal called *Romani Family*. Another organisation, The General Union of Romanies of Romania was created by a non-Romani called Lăzărescu Lăzurică who had been active since the 1920s. It was outspokenly nationalistic in orientation but survived only until 1933, managing to produce two widely distributed publications during that time, *The Romani Voice* and *The Rom*.

In October the same year in Bucharest, The General Association of Gypsies of Romania organised and held an international conference under the title United Gypsies of Europe. Its leader was Gheorghe Nicolescu, an educated Romani whose inclinations were towards integration and education for his people. In the August 1935 issue of *The Romani Voice*, he spoke of the pain of the Romani experience as motivation for change, and of the necessity of forming alliances with those free of anti-Romani prejudice:

> As long as we travel the paths of justice, honour and duty, no one and nothing can detract us from our goal, for we have with us a steadfast and loyal ally: suffering. The way towards emancipation is clear: those who care about us will be cared for in return, and we shall march together forward, ever forward.

Among other things, the conference sought to erect a monument to the abolitionist Gregory Ghica, and to make 23 December an annual Romani holiday commemorating *desrrobireja* – the emancipation from slavery. Proposals were also made for the establishment of a Romani library, hospital and university and – most important – to institute an international program of communication and cooperation among representative Romani groups everywhere, the specific aims being to strengthen the sense of ethnic solidarity, and to combat social inequality. A national Romani flag, consisting of two horizontal bars, the lower green and the upper blue, was also adopted. The event was treated with some sarcasm in the press, however, and while Martin Block, writing in Nazi Germany in the mid-1930s, mentioned it in his influential book on Romanies, he greatly minimized its significance. "Gypsies", he wrote, "offer no contribution to civilisation, and do themselves in no way help to elucidate the problem of their survival". Block's biased scholarship was used to justify Hitler's racial policies and the eventual program to annihilate the Romani population (Chapter 4).

In a chapter on Romani nationalism, Thomas Acton (1974:101) discusses the external stimuli that have affected its emergence:

> Romani nationalism has borrowed extensively from other nationalist traditions. Classical nineteenth-century nationalism, centred on the idea of a nation-state, presented to Gypsies above all the example of Zionism … More recently, "third-world nationalism", Fanonism and the Black Power writings have given a new language in which to lay claim to self-determination and cultural autonomy within someone else's power structure. This latter ideological variant is the most radical … because it makes statements about the nature of the persecuting system.

Tipler (1968:61) had already drawn attention to the model that Zionism provided for Romani nationalist sentiment, and indeed for the creation, later, of the international committee itself:

> The idea of an International Romani Committee has been inspired to a great extent by the success of Zionism, and the "philosophy of the Romani nation" as expounded by the Committee's president … is replete with references to [the] apostles of Jewish nationhood. If his example is Zionism, his bible is the UN Charter of Human Rights.

The closest thing to adopting "someone else's power structure", as Acton phrased it, was in the emergence of a Romani 'royal line' in Poland in the late 1920s, where it was particularly attractive to members of the Kwiek family, descendants of slaves liberated in Romania seventy years before. A number of Kwieks had been able to establish a dynasty and be recognised as 'kings' by local police and government officials, who even endorsed their elections. Michael Kwiek II, who succeeded his father

King Gregory in 1930, held court regularly, and in 1932 announced a pan-European tour during which he was to be accompanied by "a bodyguard of secretaries and detectives". Two years later, he announced his aim of creating a Romani state on the banks of the Ganges in India, the original homeland. This far-reaching plan was terminated when he was forced to abdicate and leave Poland by his successor, Mathias Kwiek. Mathias made a number of proposals to the Polish government for civil and social reform for the nation's Romani population, but general antigypsyism, and tensions within the Romani community over competition for the throne, resulted in little being accomplished. Among those contending were Joseph Kwiek, who had his own plan for a Romani homeland in South Africa, and Basil Kwiek, who had helped to depose King Michael. It was not until 1937 that Janusz Kwiek successfully petitioned the Archbishop of Warsaw to recognise him as king of the Romani people in the country. As a consequence, invitations were sent to various European heads of state, and he was crowned Janos I before thousands of people in the National Army Stadium, with appropriate pomp and ceremony, on July 4 of that year. At his coronation speech, delivered in Romani, he made the following pledge:

Janusz Kwiek's coronation, Warsaw, 1937

> I shall send a delegate to Mussolini asking him to grant us a piece of land in Abyssinia where Romanies can settle. Our people are weary of having had to travel throughout the ages. The time has now come for us to cease living as nomads. If the Poles will only allow us to send our children to their schools to be educated, we shall soon have out own representatives in the League of Nations.

According to a report in the *Nationalistische Landspost* for 19 March

Poster announcing Kwiek's coronation.

1937 he kept his word and approached Mussolini's fascist government to ask that Romanies be allowed to settle in an area between Somalia and Abyssinia. The following year, however, Rüdiger in Nazi Germany recommended that the Romani population be eliminated, rather than simply removed from Europe, and sterilization measures were immediately stepped up. The establishment of a Romani colony in Africa never materialized, but Janosz Kwiek's dream of representation in the League of Nations – or as it is today the United Nations – has come true. With the Nazi invasion of Poland and the policy of extermination of the Romanies, Romani unity was critically disrupted. Kwiek, as leader, was ordered to collaborate with the death squads, but refused, and was executed.

Out of the chaos following the war, Rudolf Kwiek proclaimed himself the new king, but there were few followers. With the Kwiek Dynasty no longer viable, he reappointed himself President of The World Council of Romanies, but there was no actual council, like many Romani organisations it really only existed on paper, and he died unheralded in 1964 at nearly ninety years of age. Meanwhile, some members of the Kwiek family had moved to France, where their talent for stimulating Romani political activity helped to establish a new organisation, The World Romani Community.

The only other enduring organisation to have been created before the war was in Greece, where two Romani women, who were probably of Yugoslav nationality and who then lived near Athens, established The Panhellenic Cultural Association of Greek Romanies.

During the years following the war, the Romani population in Europe was numb. Political activity was minimal and Romanies were reluctant even to identify their ethnicity publicly or draw attention to it through group effort. No reparations had been forthcoming for the Nazi atrocities committed against them, and no organised attempts had been made by any national or international agency to re-orient the survivors such as were being put into large scale effect for survivors of other victimized groups (Chapter 4); instead, pre-war anti-Romani legislation continued to operate against them. In Germany, until as late as 1947, those who had come out of the camps had to keep well hidden, or risk being incarcerated once again, this time in labour camps, if they could not produce documentation proving their German citizenship. Some of those laws remained in effect into the early 1950s, and it has come to light since then that Interpol continued to use Romani-related files originally compiled by the Nazis, in its own anti-Romani endeavours for many years after that.

Things began to move again in 1959. In that year, another Romanian Romani, Ionel Rotaru, then living in France, emerged as a leader. Taking a title from the slaveholding estates in old Wallachia, he renamed himself Vaida Voivod and attracted enough of a following among the Romani population of France to have himself acknowledged as 'The Supreme Chief of the Romani People'. He used non-Romani stereotypes to his own advantage, creating a persona for himself which attracted media attention throughout France, and an increasing following among the Romani population. Rotaru, now Voivod, established two Romani organisations: The National Romani Organisation, which was not particularly successful, and The World Romani Community, which was. The latter endeavour had input from the Kwieks, and gained support from as far afield as Poland and Canada. Rotaru drew up elaborate, nationalistic plans for the Roma, including the creation of an autonomous territory within France, and a homeland in Somalia. He sought schooling, the repeal of anti-Romani laws, the development of Romani-language literature, and war crime reparations from the German government. He founded a Romani Cultural Centre in Brussels and went so far as to have Romani passports printed.

His utopian ideals proved to be a threat to Charles de Gaulle's government, which was said to be embarrassed by Romani claims for war crimes reparations and which, in 1965, made The World Romani

Community illegal. Rotaru continued to fight, however, telling the press that "dissolution is not prohibition", and the notion of a geographical homeland, Romanestan, remained uppermost in his mind. It was important, he said, to have "a territory which would serve as a refuge in the event of persecution".

In 1965 the World Romani Community suffered a serious setback with the creation of a breakaway organisation called The International Gypsy Committee (the Komitia Lumiaki Romani). Its leader was the French Rudari Romani, Vanko Rouda (Jacques Dauvergne), whose more pragmatic approach concentrated on issues such as war crimes reparations rather than Romani passports. It established an official publication, *La Voix Mondiale Tsigane*, and stimulated the creation of affiliated bodies in other countries, such as The Gypsy Council in Britain and later on The Nordic Roma Council in Sweden. By 1972, twenty-three international organisations in twenty-two countries had been linked by the International Romani Committee. In Czechoslovakia, The Cultural Union of Roma of Slovakia, and The Union of Roma of the Czech Republic were declared illegal soon after their creation, but in the United States and Canada, Finland, Greece, Spain, Australia and elsewhere, new Romani organisations were coming into being, not as independent entities, but as members of a world-wide Romani alliance.

In 1971, the International Gypsy Committee organised the first World Romani Congress. This took place in a location near London, announced at the last minute due to threats of disruption, between 8–12 April. The event was funded in part by the World Council of Churches and the Indian Government; representatives from India and some twenty other countries were in attendance (Acton, 1974); Liégeois, 1976). At the Congress, the green and blue flag from the 1933 conference, now embellished with the red, 16-spoked chakra was reaffirmed as the national emblem of the Romani people (our flag can be ordered from *http://www.saalfrank.de*) and the anthem, *Dželem Dželem*, since sung at all congresses, adopted. This was a traditional Romani song, with new words written for it by the late Žarko Jovanović and sung by Esma Redžepova.

At that congress, the use of ethnic labels for our people which are of non-Romani origin, such as Gypsy, Zigeuner, Gitano, etc., was condemned; the organisation itself was re-named the Comité International Rom. Vanko Rouda was reconfirmed as its President, and its aims were expressed by congress chairman, Slobodan Berberski:

> The goal of this congress is to unite Romanies throughout the world, and move them to action; to bring about emancipation as we see it, and according to our own ideals; to advance at our own speed.

The International Rom Committee became the permanent secretariat and executive authority presiding over the congress. Its first task was to create five standing commissions: Social Affairs, War Crimes, Language Standardization, Culture and Education. From it, negotiations were successfully initiated with the Council of Europe (primarily in connection with anti-Romani legislation and free passage), and with the government of West Germany (in connection with war crimes reparations). It was in the early 1970s that The Indian Institute of Romani Studies was established at Chandigarh, in the Punjab, under the directorship of Padmashri Weer R Rishi, and the journal *Roma*, official organ of the Romani Union, commenced publication.

The second World Romani Congress took place seven years later in Geneva between 8–11 April 1978. Sixty delegates, and observers from twenty-six countries, were in attendance. It was chaired by Dr Jan Cibula, a Romani physician originally from Czechoslovakia but now living in Switzerland, and a twelve-member praesidium was appointed representing as many countries. This time, the Indian links were more heavily emphasized and better represented: the Prime Minister of the Punjab, and his Ministers of Foreign Affairs and of Education, as well as a number of other dignitaries from India came, and were instrumental in urging the Congress to apply for non-governmental status within the United Nations. Unlike the spirit of the first congress, this time factions differing ideologically were in evidence, a fact which attending journalists found confusing. Although no sense of a departure from the International Rom Committee was made evident, Vanko Rouda had opposed the organisation of the second Congress, and especially the existence of the working committee whose task it was to prepare for the next international meeting. This committee was called the Romano Internacionalno Jekhethanibe or International Romani Union, a designation that has gradually come to stand for the International Rom Committee itself.

A petition was drawn up at the Geneva congress formally requesting consultative status at the United Nations. It was presented to the NGO board of the UN in person in 1979 by a delegation consisting of

Honorary President of the Romani Union the late Yul Brynner, the present writer, Canadian Romani activist Ronald Lee and the late John Tene of Boston. By the following February, this had been granted. An earlier petition seeking recognition of the Romanies had been sent to the UN Commission on Human Rights by the International Romani Committee in 1968 but was unsuccessful.

The Third World Romani Congress took place in Göttingen between 16-20 May in 1981, with 300 delegates from over twenty countries participating. This was organised by The German Sinti League and partially supported by The Association for Threatened Peoples. The overriding theme of this meeting was the fate of Romanies in the Third Reich, but while survivors of the *Baro Porrajmos (*the Romani Holocaust) testified and a resolution was passed that the issue of reparations be tackled head-on, the German governments still refused adequately to acknowledge Romani losses under the Nazis.

Between 4-13 April 1990, the Fourth World Romani Congress took place at Serock on the outskirts of Warsaw, Poland, sponsored in part by UNESCO. The decade which followed saw ongoing confusion over leadership and organisation, stimulated in part by the extensive changes taking place in post-Communist Europe. The issues of asylum seekers and claims for compensation for Nazi atrocities created a need for Romanies to come together to dialogue more effectively with the non-Romani world. In the new Czech Republic, one of the major countries from which Romanies were fleeing, a lawyer named Emil Ščuka, former general secretary of the International Romani Union, convened the Fifth World Romani Congress in Prague between 24-28 July 2000, and was voted in as its new President.

The principal challenge to the IRU is the Roma National Congress, led by the Hamburg-based Rudko Kawczynski and which, because of its more recent formation, is not regarded as having inherited long-standing socialist perspectives on Romani matters. One criticism that the RNC levels at the International Romani Union is that it is still too Eastern European and, especially, Czech centred in its outlook. The Fifth World Romani Congress, however, also saw the creation of an international Parliament whose members are trying hard to bring the RNC and the IRU together, and some cooperation is apparent in such matters as political asylum and Nazi slave labour claims (Acton and Klímová, 2001).

There are many Romani organisations, though efforts to co-ordinate them are slow. Lack of funding and political separation have made it difficult for representatives from widely separated countries to meet; centuries of geographical isolation have caused local populations to be introspective rather than to see themselves as part of a world community sharing the same goals; the problems and priorities differ from place to place, and there is a conflict between, on the one hand, the traditional Romani hierarchy of leadership, and on the other selection of representation by closed ballot. The small intelligentsia which has emerged in recent years, and which generally serves as the link between the Romani and the non-Romani worlds, has become a target of resentment from some quarters, leading to the creation in one instance of an alliance of *phure Rroma* or 'traditional' Romanies who claim that the vast majority of the Romani population does not recognise or acknowledge their legitimacy as its true representatives, or indeed their identity as true Romanies. It is tempting perhaps to see this resistance to intra-group cooperation as an ingrained characteristic of our people; writing of the Rajputs, Salunke (1989:28) commented on the same behaviour, which he calls their

> major vice ... the main reason which does not allow them to come together and try to solve their problems. For minor disputes they never try to come together and negotiate to thrash out their problems or to resolve some reforms; the superiority of their kinsmen seems to be intolerable to them.

Nevertheless efforts continue to be made, both to organise and to establish our history and our identity, and it is likelier that having to struggle to coordinate our effort is simply due to the relative newness of having to do so, and the fact that we are still learning how. Organisations have come into being in Canada, Australia, Argentina, Brazil and elsewhere to accommodate the needs of newly-arriving Romani refugees. In 2001 representatives from several North and South American nations met in Ecuador with the intention of creating for the first time a pan-American Romani alliance; it now exists as the Council of the Kumpanias and Organisations of the Americas (*SKOKRA*). In the same year, Romanies from a number of European countries visited Delhi in India to work together with Indian colleagues to create a statement making clear the relationship between Romanies and India. A delegation of Romanies from many countries attended the World Conference Against Racism in

Durban, South Africa, in September 2001, and a petition was signed there and delivered to the United Nations asking that Romanies be recognised as a non-territorial nation with a seat and voting rights in the UN General Assembly.

Despite claims that Romani political effort and the reunification movement are non-existent, and that as a people we are unable to achieve such goals, or that such activity is 'un-Romani-like', recent developments clearly prove the contrary. But functioning as an organised people in an ever-shrinking world means rapid and quite drastic change for us, and while other nations have had centuries to do this – and still haven't got it perfect – we are having to catch up quickly, and are bound to make mistakes. There shouldn't be a double standard when judging our successes and failures. And we are ready to learn from others who have travelled the road before us.

Questions

1 Describe the gradual emergence of Romani organisations from the beginning.
2 Given what you have learnt about *Rromanipen*, what is the conflict between traditional Romani social structure and the creation of organisations patterned after non-Romani models?
3 If there is no royalty within Romani social structure, where does the idea of a 'Gypsy king' come from?
4 What agreement did the Kwiek family try to reach with the Nazis?
5 Why have there been attempts by various governments to make Romani organisations illegal?
6 How did efforts to organise re-emerge after the Second World War?

CHAPTER   THIRTEEN

Contributions, accomplishments and persons of note

"The Gypsies", Mrs Hersh said, "What culture have the Gypsies got?"
"No culture?" Adam said. "To hell with them".
"Mr Speaker", Wexler said, "May I ask you something? Because can you give
me the name of ten famous Gypsies?"

(Raphael, 1977:253–254).

In the absence of written records, we can only guess at what the Romani contributions have been to western culture. It is widely believed that the artificial fishing lure, for example, originated with us, but it is more likely that, rather than inventing new concepts, Romanies were now and again responsible for their introduction. Gunmetal, puppetry and certain musical styles and instruments such as the cimbalom and possibly even the guitar, may well have been first introduced to the Europeans by the incoming Romanies. The type of drum called a *dauli* in the Balkans and which finds a place in Romani musical ensembles is the same as the Indian *dhol*, just as the *zurna*, a kind of clarinet, has an almost identical counterpart in the Indian *nagasvarna* (Sanskrit *svarna* "tone, note" has become *sur, sar* in modern Indian languages, hence *zurna*). Is this merely coincidence, the result of a general cultural diffusion of instruments and styles throughout western Asia, or did our people bring these instruments and their names with them into Europe? It has also been suggested that certain methods of weaponry-manufacture and other metal-working techniques were first brought by Romanies into the West, and that some folktale themes were likewise spread from one part of Europe to another by Romani storytellers (Davidson, 1890, Vekerdi, 1976).

It is clear that there would be no flamenco without Romanies. While it is a composite musical form, it contains instrumental, choreographical and vocal characteristics with clear parallels in Asian styles (Leblon, 2002). Some of its distinctive features are only found among other Romani populations in other parts of Europe, such as the *cante jondo* or 'deep song' which has been compared with the *loki djili* or 'slow song' in Hungary, as well as with Sindhi musical forms in India (Baloch, 1968). The 'Gypsy scale' identified by Liszt is close to the oriental chromatic scale and exactly like the Indian *bhairava* scale (do, re^b, mi, fa$^\#$, sol, la^b, ti, do). In central Europe too, traditional Romani compositions have deeply influenced such European composers as Brahms ('*Acht Zigeunerlieder*'), Coleridge-Taylor ('*Gypsy Suite*'), Dvořák ('*Cigánské Melodie*'), Enescu ('*Romanian Rapsody*'), Dohnyani ('*Andante Rubato alla Zingaresca*'), Haydn ('*Zigeunertanz*'), Joachim ('*Alla Zingara*'), Ketelby ('*Chal Romano*'), Kreisler ('*Gypsy Caprice*'), Liszt ('*Die Drei Zigeuner*'), Mozart ('*Ungliche Liebe*'), Rachmaninoff ('*Hungarian Dance*'), Ravel ('*Tzigane*'), Rossini ('*Chanson de Zora*'), Sain-Saëns ('*Gypsy Dance*'), Sarasate ('*Zigeunerweisen*'), Schubert ('*Gretchen*'), Verdi ('*La Zingara*'), Wolf ('*Die Zigeunerin*') and numbers of others. Certain musical features such as use of the bhairava scale, melisma, etc. appear to have their roots in India, certainly modified by Middle Eastern styles acquired in Anatolia before being first introduced into Europe in the fourteenth century.

Klezmer music, currently enjoying great popularity, has at least some of its origins in Romani tradition, according to Israeli scholar Mirel Reznić, whose research reveals that "many of the internationally-known Hassidic tunes created in Eastern Europe have their roots firmly planted in Gypsy culture" (Hoffman, 1988:5). The generous representation of musicians in the following list of prominent individuals testifies to the significance of this profession, one of the few that allowed Romanies to make a living in the non-Romani world.

While there are many individuals of Romani descent who have become prominent not only in their own countries but internationally, success in the non-Romani world should not always be seen as the true measure of accomplishment. The real bringers of change are those who count as prominent figures *within* the Romani community, not only those who have made a mark outside it. Nevertheless, there are many descended from Romani families who have acquired prominence and who are regarded with pride by Romanies. There is, of course, a distinct difference between those who have come out of a Romani home life, and who consciously identify as Romanies, and those who have Romani ancestry but who otherwise have never had any contact with that world.

It is common for us to talk about whether this or that well-known individual is of Romani descent. Many names come up repeatedly, among them John Bunyan, Yul Brynner, Mother Teresa, Pablo Picasso, Sir Richard Burton, Elvis Presley, Ava Gardener and Clark Gable, but there is no hard evidence to prove this one way or the other. More disturbing is the fact that there are numbers of personalities who know they are of Romani ancestry, but who deliberately keep that fact a secret. Such people could use their prominence to help speak for the Romani cause, but such is their fear of prejudice that they choose to keep quiet instead. Others who have mentioned it in print at the beginning of their careers, have pushed it into the background as they have become better known to the general public; perhaps one day all individuals of Romani ancestry will declare that fact openly, and with pride.

The following list could easily be twice as long; several contemporary political figures have been omitted, for example, particularly if their names appear elsewhere in the book. Among those who are noteworthy are:

Sidonie

Sidonie Adlersberg, who was a Sinti child who had been adopted by the non-Romani family of Breirather in 1935 in Garsten, Germany, and brought up as their own, unaware of her ethnic background. In 1943 the police came to her home and took her away. She was sent to Auschwitz-Birkenau on the last transport and was murdered there. A documentary film was made of her story in 1991.

Rafael, *Miguel* and *Maria Albaicín*, siblings who each appeared in different films produced in Spain: Rafael as a bullfighter in *Maria Antonia, La Fiesta Sigue* and *La Caramba*, Miguel as a dancer in *El Amor Brujo* and Maria as a performer in *La Fuente Magica, Los Pianos Mecanicos* and *Café de Chinitas*.

Carmen Amaya, born in 1920 in Granada but moved to the United States to escape the Spanish Civil War, where she became well-known as a flamenco artist.

Valentin Bagalaenko, a singer and equestrian artist from the Ukraine who travelled with the Russian Teatr Romen and who has made a number of commercial recordings.

Maria Bako, a film actress from Hungary, who appeared in Silvio Soldini's film *Una Alma Dividita in Due*; she was unable to attend the 1993 Venice Film Festival after immigration authorities refused her entry into Italy because of her ethnicity.

Jánosz Balász, born in Alsó Kubin, Hungary in 1905, known for his naive art and poetry. When his work became known he quickly gained a high reputation among artists. It has been presented at various independent exhibitions, as well as at an international exhibition of Romani artists in Budapest, in 1979. He died in 1977.

Kálmán Balogh, a renowned cimbalom-player born in 1959 in Miskolc in Hungary. He teaches the instrument today.

Lord Berners

Veijo Baltzar, was born in 1942 in Finland, and has written a number of novels including *Polttava Vie*, *Verikihlat*, *Mari* and *Phuro*. He is a civil rights activist and has written about the condition of Romanies in his own country.

Lord Gerald Berners was born in 1883 in Shropshire, England and reportedly had Romani ancestry on his mother's side. In the 1920s he served as Honorary Attaché to the British Diplomatic Service in Constantinople, and later in Rome. He wrote an opera and several ballets, the best known of which was *The Triumph of Neptune*, though he is better remembered for his eccentric behaviour, which often brought media attention. He died in 1950.

János Bihári, born in 1764 in Hungary, a virtuoso violinist from the county of Pozsony (Bratislava). He composed music especially in the stirring *verbunkos* style, which was used to rally new recruits to enlist in the army, and which was later incorporated into the compositions of Franz Liszt. He died in 1827.

Vera Bílá, a citizen of the Czech Republic, sang with her violinist father until she was twenty-five, when she was heard by Nerez, one of the country's leading folk groups, which asked her to join them. She now has her own ensemble, *Kale*, consisting mostly of family members, and has made an impact all over Europe and North America. She made several commercial recordings, and was the subject of a documentary film called *Black, White and in Colour* (1998).

Sylvester Boswell was a Romanichal author born in the 1890s in Lancashire who served in the British army during the First World War. His autobiography, *The Book of Boswell*, appeared in 1970.

Hristo Botev was born in Kalofer, Bulgaria, in 1848. He studied in Odessa where he wrote a dissertation on the Russian Democratic Revolution, then moving to Romania where he worked as a publicist and published various collections of poetry. He returned to Bulgaria, where he was involved in the effort to free that country from Ottoman domination. He died in mysterious circumstances in 1876.

James Buchanan Brady, '*Diamond Jim*', was born in 1856 reportedly to a Romanichal mother. His first job was as a hotel bellboy and messenger, afterwards working at various jobs for a railway company. He then worked for a railroad supply company and began converting his pay into precious stones. Through his trading skills he gradually collected many sets of jewelry becoming a millionaire while still a young man. He donated generously to the Johns Hopkins Hospital and founded the Brady Urological Institute in Baltimore. He died in 1917.

Michael Caine, born Maurice Micklewhite in 1933, descends on his father's side from South London Romani horse traders. An actor in such films as *Educating Rita*, *Goldmember* and *The Actors*. He received a knighthood in 2000.

Antonio Cansino, created Spanish dance as it is known today, by combining the classical tradition with Romani flamenco. His most famous dance was the *bolero*, which swept the world. His son, Eduardo was brought to America by the wealthy Stuyvesant family and became the pet of New York society; he married a dancer from the Ziegfield Follies, and had a daughter, Rita (*Hayworth*; *q.v.*).

Charlie Chaplin was born in England in 1889, and died in 1977. He was mainly famous as a comic character actor, though he also appeared in such serious classics as *Limelight*. His mother's people were the Romanichal Smiths. He spent as much

Charlie Chaplin

time as he could in Romani company, and reportedly modeled his 'tramp' character on his perceptions of Romani life. His sympathy for the treatment of Romanies in Nazi Germany also led to his playing a Hitler look-alike in *The Great Dictator* (1940).

William Clinton, president of the United States between 1993–2001, was formerly named William Blythe. He is descended from the brother of the Romani leader Charles Blythe, who was crowned 'King of the Scottish Gypsies' at Kirk Yetholm in 1847, and whose brother Andrew emigrated to America. Andrew's son, Andrew Jefferson Blythe, died in 1860 and was President Clinton's great-great-great grandfather.

József Choli Daróczi, a well-known writer from Hungary, who has translated the four gospels and Lorca's *Romancero Gitano*, among other pieces, into Romani.

David Essex, whose real name is Albert Cook, is a British actor and recording artist born in 1947, who has played the part of Christ in the stage-play *Godspell* and of Che Guevara in *Evita*. He is the patron of the Gypsy Council for Education, Culture, Welfare and Civil Rights.

Tera Fabiánová was born in Czechoslovakia in 1930 and was one of the first authors in that country to publish in the Romani language.

Philomena Franz was born in 1922 in Biberach an der Rug and today

lives in Rösrath near Cologne. For seven years she made her living as a folkloric dancer and singer in a theater group. In 1943 she was deported to the concentration camps at Ravensbrück, Oranienburg and Auschwitz-Birkenau. She writes mostly Romani tales and organises literary readings at schools and universities. In August 1995 she was awarded the 'Federal Cross of Merit', the first Sinti to be awarded this prize, the highest civil award that Germany confers.

Tony Gatlif, an Algerian-born film producer now resident in France, known for his Romani-themed films, including *Les Princes*, *Corre Gitano*, *Latcho Drom*, *Gadjo Dilo*, *Mondo* and *Vengo del Mora*.

Tony Gatlif

Alexander German, who in Russia in the 1920s led the All-Russian Union of Gypsies and translated numbers of Russian texts into Romani, as well as writing his own original material.

Rita Hayworth, born Margarita Carmen Cansino in 1918, was the granddaughter of **Antonio Cansino**, *q.v.*, whose son Eduardo (her father) opened a dancing school in Hollywood in 1926. It was here that she first entered show business. She is best known for her appearance in such films as *The Dancing Pirate* (1936), *The Loves of Carmen* (1948), *Circus World* (1964) and *The Rover* (1967).

Rita Hayworth

Patricio Lafcadio Hearn was born in 1850 in Greece to a Cypriot Romani mother and a British father who was descended from the Romanichal Hearns (Herons). He was educated in America, and was particularly interested in the Creole population of Louisiana, where he ran afoul of the law by marrying an African American woman. He was one of the first to establish the modern-day journalistic style of writing. He left the United States for Japan, where he died in 1904.

Tomáš Holomek, born in 1911, a former Member of Parliament and co-founder of the Union of Roma. Holomek was also the first-ever Romani lawyer in the former Czechoslovakia. He devoted most of his professional life to the Romani movement and died in 1988.

Miroslav Holomek was born in 1925 in Svatobožice near Kyjov and co-founded the Union of Roma, eventually becoming its president in 1969. He was much influenced by the activities of his uncle Tomáš. He spent his life working for Romanies, in particular trying to improve the dialogue between Romanies and the majority population in the former Czechoslovakia, and died in 1989.

Bob Hoskins is a film actor who was born in England in 1942. His mother's family is Sinti, from Germany. He made one film with a supposedly Romani theme, *The Raggedy Rawney* (1990 – rawney means 'woman' in the Romanichal dialect, in Common Romani *rani*), but he is better known for his appearance in such films as *Last Orders*, *Mona Lisa*, *Brazil*, *Roger Rabbit*, *Hook* and *The Cotton Club*.

Wladislaw Jakowicz was born in Krakow in 1915. This writer and dancer left Poland for Russia where he stayed for the entire period of the Second World War, afterwards settling in Sweden, where he wrote the poem-story *O Thari thaj e Zerfi* that was published in 1981.

Sandra Jayat, a cousin of ***Django Reinhardt***, q.v., was born into a Manouche family in Italy, subsequently moving to Paris, where she worked as a commercial artist. She has published her poetry and exhibited her art extensively, and in 1992 designed a postage stamp commemorating Romanies. She has written an autobiographical novel, *La Longue Route d'une Zingarina* (1974), was 1972 recipient of the Children's Literature Prize (France) and the 1978 recipient of the Poetry Book Prize (Sweden).

Žarko Jovanovič, a musician from Serbia who composed the words for the Romani national anthem *Dželem Dželem*, and who made many gramophone recordings before his death in 1997.

Šaip Jusuf, a Macedonian scholar who has written extensively on aspects of Romani grammar, and who published a full-length grammar of the language in 1980. He had already published a biography of Tito (in Romani) in 1978. In its early days he was also active in the establishment of the International Romani Union.

Sonya Kavalevsky became the first-ever female university professor in Sweden in 1884. She taught mathematics at Stockholm University.

Usin Kerim, born in 1928, was one of the earliest Bulgarian Romanies to publish poetry. His first book was *Gilja la Cehratar* ('Songs from the Tent'), which appeared in 1955.

Vania de Gila Kochanowski, a Holocaust survivor from Latvia now living in France, he holds two doctoral degrees and has written widely on aspects of Romani grammar and history. His best-known works are *Gypsy Studies* (1963), *Romano Atmo* (1992), *Parlons Tsigane* (1994) and *Le Roi des Serpents* (1996).

Elena Lacková from Slovakia wrote a play, *Horiaci Cigansky Tabor* ("*The Gypsy Camp is Burning*") that was published in 1947, and has continued writing ever since, most recently the widely acclaimed *A False Dawn* (1999). She is president of the Cultural Association of Citizens of Romani Nationality in Slovakia.

Birelli Lagrene, recording artist born in 1966 into a Sinti family in Alsace, France, he began playing the guitar when he was four, and jazz when he was only seven years old, at first imitating **Django Reinhardt** but later developing his own distinctive guitar style. His father Fiso was also a guitarist of note.

Jem Mace, a British Romanichal born in Norfolk in 1831, who held the national championship for bare-knuckle fighting. Known as 'the father of modern boxing', he established the Marquis of Queensbury rules and boxing with gloves. He died in 1910.

Leksa Manuš (**Alexander Belugins**), a poet and translator born in

Moscow in 1949. He translated the Indian classic the *Ramayana* into Romani, which was published in India in 1990, and edited a volume of Romani poetry. He died in 1997 at the age of 48.

'La Liance' was a famous Romani dancer in seventeenth century French society. She was painted by the artist Beaubrun, but went into mourning for the rest of her life after her husband was arrested and hanged for highway robbery.

Ceferino Jiménez Malla, *'El Pelé'* was born into a Spanish Caló family in 1861, Ceferino never went to school, nor learned to read or write. Although he made his living as a horse dealer, he was devoted to teaching the doctrines of the Roman Catholic Church to the Romani community. He was persecuted for defending a priest during the Spanish Civil War, but refused when offered his freedom, thus he was shot to death in 1936. The church canonized him as a martyr in 1997.

Matéo Maximoff, born in Barcelona, Matéo was a well-known Kalderash Vlax writer who lived in France where his ancestors, metalworkers from Russia, had settled at the end of the nineteenth century. He wrote in French as well as in his native Romani, and his first work, *Les Ursitory* (1946), has been translated into fourteen languages. Some of his other books include *La Septième Fille, Condamné à Survivre, Savina* and *Vinguerka*. In 1964

Matéo Maximoff

he was ordained a pastor, and in 1994 he published a translation of the New Testament in the Kalderash dialect. He died in 1999.

Max Miller, of music hall fame, was born in Brighton in the south of England in 1894. His family were Romanichals on his father's side, and were circus people. He left school at twelve and at the age of 20 joined the army, where he first developed his talents as an entertainer. He went on to perform at the London Palladium, and appeared in 14 films, including *Good Companions* (1933), *The Good Old Days* (1937) and *Asking for Trouble* (1942). His ribald humour, though tame by today's standards, got him banned from BBC radio for five years. He died in 1963.

Bruno Morelli, a self-taught portrait artist born in 1958 in Italy, who has had many exhibits and who organised the first and second Mondiale d'Arte delle Zingari.

Lazăr Năftănăilă established 'The Brotherhood of New Farmers' in the 1920s for agricultural Romanies in Transylvania, with the purpose of promoting cultural and political awareness. In 1933 he started the journal *Neamul Ţiganesc* ("*The Romani People*").

Cinka Panna was born in 1711 into a musical family in Gömör in what is today Slovakia, and played first violin in her own ensemble. Her family jointly composed the famous piece *Rákoczi*, among many others. Several Hungarian writers and composers, such as Jókai Mór, Kodáli Zoltán and Dozsa Endre have adopted her style in their own works. She has been commemorated in an annual festival in Gemer County since 1970 and has been honoured on a postage stamp. She died in 1772.

Ivo Papasov was born in 1952 in Kurdžali in Bulgaria. Starting with the accordion, he switched to the clarinet early on, later forming the ensemble *Trakija* that specialised in wedding music, and soon became the highest-paid wedding musician in the country, couples even arranging the dates of their marriages in order to have him available to play.

Šakir Pašov edited a Romani journal and an founded an organisation both called *Istikbal* ("*Future*") in Bulgaria in the 1920s; after the Second World War he created a new Romani organisation and became a member of Parliament, but was imprisoned in Belen by the Communists for promoting Romani ethnic nationalism.

Alexander Petrovič, born at the beginning of the twentieth century in Yugoslavia, as just a boy he helped care for victims of dysentery in Russia during the First World War. Throughout the 1920s he was medical assistant at the University of Odessa. He was murdered by an unknown person in 1942.

Manitas de Plata, whose family name is ***Ballardo*** (sometimes spelt ***Baliardo***) was born in southern France and became one of the best-known commercial flamenco guitarists in the 1950s, helping to establish an international following for this music.

Freddie Prinze, a television actor, was born Frederick Karl Pruetzel in San Juan in 1954 of Hungarian Romani and Puerto Rican parents. He is best remembered for his role in the comedy series *Chico and the*

Freddie Prinze

Man. He died by committing suicide in 1977 but his son, Freddie Prinze Jr, continues his acting tradition.

Juan de Dios Ramírez Heredia was originally a social worker among his people but became interested in politics early on, eventually being elected to the Spanish Parliament. He has since become a member of the Brussels-based European Parliament. He represents the Union Romani based in Barcelona and has revived a variety of inflected Romani for the Calé in Spain.

Stefan Razvan was the son of a slave and a free woman in sixteenth century Moldavia, where he became ruler of that principality in April 1595. He was deposed four months later and murdered in December the same year.

Esma

Esma Redžepova is probably the best-known Romani singer, whose vocal range and emotive delivery can bring tears to a whole audience. She comes from Skopje in Macedonia and has made many recordings, including the Romani national anthem *Dželem Dželem*, with which she opened the First World Romani Congress in England in 1971. In 2002 the International Romani Union nominated her for consideration for a Nobel Prize.

***Jean-Baptiste Reinhardt*, '*Django*'**, a French Manush   Django
born in Germany, Django was one of the greatest-ever composers of jazz music and is considered to be the founder of Romani jazz interpretation. During his youth he travelled through Italy, France, Belgium and Algeria and later visited America. He played constantly, despite never having learned to read music. At the age of eighteen he lost two fingers and was forced to create a completely new technique of playing with only three fingers. A number of other prominent musicians, B B King and Duke Ellington among them, have credited Django Reinhardt for their inspiration. He died in 1953, leaving a musical legacy that continues to grow.

Schukenack Reinhardt, a Sinti Romani born in Weinsberg, Germany in 1921 who studied at the Mainz Conservatory. With his quartet he became a prominent Jazz violinist in the style of ***Django Reinhardt***, q.v., whose performances are heard in his four-volume record set *Musik Deutscher Zigeuner*. He was deported to Poland by the Nazis in 1943 but survived the Holocaust.

Pierre de la Roche was a famous eighteenth century wood-carver who was commissioned by the king of France to create the ornamentation on the royal ships in the port of Rochefort. He died in his eighties in Touraine.

Rodney Smith, 'Gipsy Smith' was an evangelist, born in England in 1860. His preaching style was reportedly so powerful that he could easily draw a crowd of ten thousand. He published many religious tracts and made numbers of sound recordings of himself singing hymns; his autobiography, *Gipsy Smith: His Life and Work* was published in 1902. He died in 1947.

Antonio Solario, 'Il Zingaro', a metal-smith, was born in Italy in 1382 (forty years before the generally assumed date of the first arrival of Romanies in that country); he asked to marry the daughter of artist Colantonio del Fiore who, in an effort to get rid of him told him he

Settela

could only marry her if he could paint her portrait as well as he himself could. Solario went away and studied art, later to return and successfully claim his bride. His paintings, including a self-portrait, are to be seen in Italy, both in Latrano and in the Convent of Saint Severino in Naples. He died in 1455.

Melanie Spitta, a German-born Sinti, has done much to bring public attention to the Porrajmos through her documentary films, which include *Das Falsche Wort* and *Wir Sind Sintikinder und Nicht Zigeuner.*

Settela Steinbach was the Dutch Sinti girl whose haunting face is gazing through the door of a transport waggon that left Amsterdam on 19 May 1944 for Auschwitz and Bergen-Belsen, and from which she never returned. She has become an enduring symbol of the Holocaust, and was the subject of a documentary film produced in the Netherlands in 1994.

Ljatif Sucuri, a true Romani hero, was born at the beginning of the First World War in Yugoslavia. During the Albanian fascist occupation of that region during the Second World War, he petitioned the chief of police repeatedly to intervene to stop the killing of Romanies, which he did by denying to the Nazis that there were any Romanies in the area. He was denounced by the collaborators to the partisans, and was abducted and shot in 1945.

Ferencz Sztojka was a late nineteenth century writer in Hungary, where he was born, who compiled the first dictionary of the Romani language to be written by a native speaker, which was published in 1886, an extensive though little-known work surely deserving republication.

Rosa and ***Katarina Taikon***, Kalderash sisters born in 1926 and 1932 respectively in Tibrö, Sweden, who travelled with their family until the age of ten. They were not allowed to attend school, obtaining their education wholly within the Romani community. Today, Rosa is a silversmith who makes jewelry much in demand throughout Scandinavia. Her first exhibition was in 1969. Katarina became famous for her writing, especially children's books, and she also published the journal *Zigenaren* ('*The Romani*'), lectured extensively and published articles on the situation of the Romanies in Sweden. She died in 1995.

Trollman in real life, and the caricature of him in the German press emphasizing his 'non-Aryan' features.

Johann Wilhelm Trollman, 'der Ruckelle' was a Sinti born in Germany in 1906. He became the light-heavyweight national champion on 9 June 1933 when he fought the German Adolf Wilt for that title. Because the Nazis could not tolerate a German's being defeated by a Romani, the match was mocked in the press, Trollmann being accused of using 'Gypsy trickery' to win and a rematch was held on June 17 at which he appeared, this time with his hair dyed blond, and stood still while Wilt easily beat him. He was deported to the concentration camp at Neuengamme in 1942 and was shot there the following year.

Raya

Rajsa Udovikova, '*Raya*', is one of the foremost Romani performers in

"Papusza"

Europe. She began as an actress with the Teatr Romen in Moscow, moving to Oslo after marrying a Norwegian and developing her career as a musician and singer. She collects traditional Romani music that she plays on her seven-stringed guitar, and has performed and recorded in London, Athens, Amsterdam, Paris, Beirut and Delhi. Her daughter **Natasha** continues the family tradition.

Averian Vojtiexovski ran the Romani School in Leningrad during the 1930s but was executed by the Soviet authorities in 1938 for what they claimed were anti-government activities.

Bronisława Wajs, 'Papusza'. A poet with more than thirty collections to her name Papusza, who was born in 1910, was a source of strength and hope for Romanies during the Second World War, when she survived by hiding in the forests. She wrote about this experience in her book *Krwawe Łzy ("Bloody Tears"* – its subtitle was "What we endured under the Nazis in Volhynia in '43 and '44"). Sadly, she was shunned by many Polish Romanies for revealing too much of the culture to the outside world. Her works were published by Julian Tuwim, Jerzy Ficowski, and others. She died in 1987.

Yuri Yunakov was born in Haskovo, Bulgaria of Turkish Romani ancestry, teaching himself the *kaval* (a wooden flute) before he was ten, then the clarinet and saxophone. He became Bulgaria's leading exponent of Romani music, moving to the United States in 1994.

Josef Zawinul, 'Joe'. Jazz pianist born in Vienna in 1932 to a Sinti mother, Joe Zawinul emigrated to the United States in 1959 and has played with such greats as Dinah Washington, Cannonball Adderly and Miles Davis. He wrote the jazz standard *Birdland* and numerous other pieces, including the symphony *Stories of the Danube*.

Questions

1 Is there a 'Romani music'?
2 Name six prominent people of Romani descent.
3 Papusza did a great deal to bring the Romani experience to the world, yet she was shunned by her own people because of it. Discuss.

CHAPTER FOURTEEN

Amari Čhib: Our language

Amara čhibasa, varekajgodi šaj tradas and'e ljumja
"With our language, we can travel anywhere in the world"

Romani is a powerful factor of our identity. A saying exists that *Amari čhib s'amari zor* "our language is our strength", and it was believed for a long time that no one except Romanies could speak it – if you knew Romani, you must *be* Romani, because what outsider would ever want to learn it or even have the opportunity to do so? That is not the case any longer, and there are now summer schools offering courses in the language to anybody who is interested. It is also believed by many Romanies that if you *don't* speak it, you have lost your identity: the late Matéo Maximoff said in a 1994 interview in *Jekh Čhib* that "Wer kein Romanes mehr spricht, ist kein Rom mehr" ("whoever no longer speaks Romani, is no longer a Romani"). This is not true nor is it really fair since some populations, e.g. in Spain and Hungary, have lost the language through legislation and not by choice. But it demonstrates the depth of feeling that can exist.

Something should be said concerning two common misassumptions about Romani; first that it is not a written language, and second that great efforts are made to prevent outsiders from learning it.

Not counting early word-lists and grammars written by non-Romanies that date as far back as the 1500s, Romani has been written by Romanies for about a century in different periodicals. Not all in the same dialect or orthography of course, but taken together, the corpus of the written language from the early 1900s onward is considerable. Romani families in the USA have kept letters in Romani, written in the Cyrillic alphabet, sent by relatives left behind in Russia a hundred years ago, and bibles and portions of the gospels have been published in it for nearly as long. But the past decade especially has seen a virtual outpouring of publications in our language, not only in the dozens of magazines and newspapers which exist but in translations of various literary works, books of original poetry, formal documents relating to human rights and other organisations, and so on.

The withholding of our language from non-Romanies is truer for some groups than for others. Speakers of Sintitska for example are much more protective of it than speakers of, say, Kalderashitska, and they have been successful in getting books on the language removed from libraries. This attitude is understandable, since in the Sintis' experience in Germany especially, outsiders have tried to learn it for entirely the wrong reasons. But confusing even well intentioned investigators has a long tradition, as some of the first word lists, which contain innocently collected false and vulgar Romani equivalents, show. The fact remains that there are now hundreds of grammars and dictionaries of Romani – including Sintitska – and these are accessible for anyone really wanting to find them. There are even language-learning tapes available for purchase. It is also the case that with our increased participation in world affairs, with Romani NGO representation at the United Nations, and with the Internet linking us as never before, we *need* a modern, efficient language. Keeping it hidden isn't possible, nor does doing so help us interact with each other globally.

For centuries, our Romani language puzzled Europeans. It sounded like nothing they were familiar with, and yet it contained words they recognised from their own languages. This led some to speculate that it was an invented, secret jargon and not a real language at all. But of course it is a real language, and a rich and complex one, descending from Sanskrit, just as Italian and French descend from Latin.

The reason that it contains words from European languages is because it began in India as a military lingua franca, which has been given the name *Rajputic* (see Chapter 1). Everyone who spoke it had his own mother tongue and there were dozens of those; they only used 'Rajputic' as a common means of communication while in the army camps. As the migration moved further away from India, this military lingua franca continued to be used, because the soldiers and their camp followers remained together and were obliged to continue speaking it as the only language they had in common. It was composed of Indian and Dardic and Persian and Kurdish words, and was taken through Armenia into the Byzantine Empire, where Greek was the main language, and where Armenian and Greek and Georgian and Ossetic words were added to the vocabulary. Its originally Indian grammar was also being supplemented by grammar from these other languages, but most especially from mediaeval Greek. By this time, new generations were learning it as a first language, and so Romani was born. But the subsequent move into Europe took place over seven centuries ago, before even the Europeans knew about physics or chemistry or capitalism or computers; like German or Bulgarian or Hungarian at that time, Romani had no words for these concepts, which did not yet exist. As Romanies encountered aspects of European culture that were new to them, they used the words they heard and incorporated them into Romani. Just as English and French people first learned about science from contact with the Islamic world, and adopted words from Arabic such as 'chemistry', 'algebra', 'zero', 'alkali', 'alcohol', 'zenith' and so on, Romanies too acquired the words we needed and added them to our language. The Rajputs didn't leave India with words for 'television' or 'automobile'! Less than a third of the entries in the *Oxford English Dictionary* are original English words but come instead from Latin and French and a host of other languages; Romani actually has a higher proportion of its own native vocabulary than has English.

Sociologists recognise that people's attitudes to a particular language or dialect are really a reflection of how they feel about the people who speak it. And if Romanies are not held in high esteem, then our language cannot possibly be. It has been said very often that Romani is a poor language, with few words and even fewer of them able to express abstract or philosophical notions. This is not true and is a statement usually originating with people who cannot speak it.

Romani took shape and came together in Anatolia, where the Romani population stayed for two centuries or more. There is some evidence that the journey from there into Europe didn't happen all at once, but that there were different movements up into the Balkans and beyond at different times. For example the Istriani Romanies in Slovenia have very little Greek influence in their speech, suggesting that their ancestors went into Europe not long after their arrival in Byzantine lands. As Fraser's work has demonstrated (in Chapter 1), it was here that we find the beginnings of the distinct dialect divisions; the ancestors of the speakers of those found across the north of Europe, which include Sinti Romani, seem to have left Anatolia at a different time, and perhaps under different circumstances, from those whose descendants speak Vlax Romani today. Baltic and other northern dialects lack the extensive West Slavic, Romanian and Hungarian influences which are so typical of Vlax.

There are four main dialect groups: Southern (or Balkan), Vlax (or Danubian), Central and Northern. One example of a Southern dialect is Drindari, spoken in Bulgaria. Vlax dialects, such as Kalderash or Lovari Romani, are spoken by people descended from the slaves freed from the Romanian estates in the nineteenth century (Chapter 2); the Central dialects include some of those spoken in Slovakia, Hungary and elsewhere, such as Bashaldo, while the Northern dialects include Sinti, Baltic, Finnish Kaalo Romani and the now-extinct dialects of Britain and the Iberian Peninsula. In some places in Europe, particularly in Britain, Spain, Scandinavia and parts of the Balkans, the original Romani has blended to such an extent with the surrounding European language that all it retains is the vocabulary, used in the grammatical framework of the local non-Romani language.

As with other languages, Romani must be cultivated if we are going to be able to use it in international situations. Where there are national standards for, say, Czech or Polish or Macedonian, which are monitored by governmental bodies expressly created as 'guardians of the language', the equivalent is only now becoming a reality for Romani.

An especial problem is that Romani exists in many dialects – sixty or more – and creating a standardized variety which most of their speakers will understand and support, is a huge task. There are two possibilities: to create an entirely new, composite written form with features from all of the dialect groups, or to take a dialect which already exists and which already has many speakers, and teach it everywhere once we have schools to make that possible. The dialects of those groups whose ancestors were slaves in Wallachia and Moldavia (the Vlax dialects) meet both these criteria; they have the greatest number of speakers – perhaps half of all Romani spoken – and they are found all over the world. At our international meetings, those present whose native Romani is not Vlax will often adjust to Vlax as the common dialect; prominent individuals from non-Vlax families such as Orhan Galjuš or Hristo Kjučukov or Horvath Aládár nevertheless use Vlax in public discourse. The present writer began learning Vlax only as a young adult. But already there are objections from representatives speaking other kinds of Romani, more often on subjective rather than objective grounds; from spokesmen from the Baltic group, for instance. Until a consensus is reached, publications will continue to appear in a variety of dialects and a variety of different spellings.

Romani vocabulary

No single dialect has retained every original word or grammatical feature. Some dialects have lost useful words along the way and either use another Romani word to make up for it or have taken in a new word from outside. Thus while many dialects have kept separate words for 'tree' and 'wood' (*rukh* and *kašt*), and for 'say' and 'tell' (*phen-* and *phuker-*), the words for 'tree' and 'tell' have been lost in the Vlax dialects, which have now generalized *kašt* and *phen-* respectively for both words. The original grammatical rule for creating comparative adjectives with the ending *-eder* (*cikno* 'small', *cikneder* 'smaller') has been lost altogether in some dialects, which instead express this with words adopted from European languages: *maj cikno, meg cikno*. Nevertheless, if a list were made of all the thematic words in all of the sixty or more dialects, the native vocabulary would be a rich one, and this is something that will have to be done in creating a common Romani, which will have separate words for 'say' and 'tell' and 'wood' and 'tree', and for many other concepts often expressed using non-Romani vocabulary. Romani also has many productive endings that can be used to create new words. Thus the suffixes *-pen* (which is Indian) and *-mos* (which is Greek) can make nouns out of other parts of speech; from the word *šaj*, used with verbs to express 'can' or 'able' might come the new words *šajipen* 'ability' and *šajimos* 'possibility'. The word for 'impossible' could be similarly derived from *šaj*: *biša-jutno*. From *našti* 'cannot' could be made *naštipen* 'impossibility' and *naštivalo* 'incapable'. From *pes* and *pen* 'himself', 'themselves' can be made *peskerimasko* 'selfish' or *pengeripen* 'self-determination'. The word-building potential of Romani is tremendous, and it is fair to say that there is no concept that potentially cannot be adequately expressed in the language. But it requires cultivation and this can only come with the support and interest not only of our own people, whose priorities too often involve food, housing and employment rather than grammars and alphabets, but of the societies among whom we live.

Samples of the language: some useful phrases

How are you?	*Sar san? Sar maj san?*
	So keres? So maj keres?
Fine, thanks	*Mišto, najis Devleske!*
Congratulations! (to a male)	*T'aves baxtalo!*
(to a female)	*T'aves baxtali!*
(to a group)	*T'aven baxtale!*
Thank you! (to one person)	*Najis tuke!*
	Parikerav tut!
(to more than one)	*Najis tumenge!*
	Parikerav tumen!
You're welcome!	*Naj pala soste!*
	Khančeske!
Goodbye (to one leaving)	*Dža Devlesa!*
(to one staying)	*Ačh Devlesa!*
	Mukhav tut e Devlesa!
What's your name?	*Sar bučhos? Sar bučhos tuke?*
My name is _____ (man)	*Me bučhov (man) o _____*
(woman)	*Me bučhov (man) e _____*
Where do you live?	*Kaj bešes?*
Where are you from?	*Katar aves?*
What country are you from?	*Anda savo them aves?*
Is your family with you?	*Tjiri familija si vi tusa?*
Where are you going?	*Kaj džas?*
Can I help you?	*Šaj žutiv tut?*
What kind of work do you do?	*Savatar butji keres?*
	Soski butji keres?
	Če fjalo butji keres?
I don't understand you.	*Či hatjerav tut. Či haljerav tut.*
Do you understand me?	*Hatjeres man? Haljeres man?*

Come with me	*T'aves mansa; hajde mansa*
Let's go together	*Kethanes džastar*
Let's get a cup of coffee	*Te pjas kafa*
How? Why? Where? When?	*Sar? Anda soste? Kaj? Kana?*
Here. There.	*Kathe. Kothe.*
Yes. No.	*Va. Na.*

Samples of the language: some proverbs

While Romani has only been written to any great extent since the twentieth century, it is very rich in oral tradition, and the first Romani-language publication in fact appeared about a hundred years ago. There are many volumes of Romani folktales (see for example Mode, 1984 and Tong, 1989). Proverbs and maxims also abound – it is through these that wisdom is codifed, and the rules of social behaviour are passed from generation to generation. They are called *garade lava* or 'hidden words' in Romani because their meaning is not always apparent. The following are in the Vlax Romani dialect:

Na le tjiri kher te ličhares e pori la sapnjaki; punrranges si te ličhares lako šero
"Don't use your boot to crush a snake's tail; you can crush its head with your bare foot" (If you don't do a job properly, no amount of preparation will make it succeed).

Kon phenela o čačipe, musaj leske te thol pesko punrro and'e kakali
"Whoever (is about to) tell the truth should have his foot in the stirrup" (The truth can hurt people and make them angry; get ready to run).

So arakhes tu and'o dorjavo telal, musaj sas t'avilo and'o dorjavo opral
"What you find downstream must have come from upstream" (You don't know what someone has done before you knew him; be careful, the past has consequences).

Našti garaves muca ande gono, lake vundžja ka-sitjaren-pe
"You can't hide a cat in a sack, its claws will show themselves (through it)" (The truth will eventually reveal itself).

Maj kuč ekh šošoj ande tigaja de sar šov and'o veš
"A rabbit in the pot is better than six in the woods" (Certainty is better than speculation).

Le sama e gavestar kaj či bešen džukle
"Be careful in the village where there are no dogs" (All villages have dogs, so if there is a village where there aren't any, something must be very wrong. A cautionary saying).

Te manges te dikhes e mačhen, na hamosar o pani
"If you want to see the fish, don't stir up the water" (Approach the situation carefully, don't be rough or hasty).

Te ala mangel o Del, vi daži del puške ekh matora
"If God wished it, even a broomstick could shoot bullets" (All things are possible with God).

Dorango džukel merela bokhatar
"A dog with two masters will die from hunger" (You can't divide your loyalty; each master will assume that the other one has fed the dog).

Maj kali e mura, maj gulo a'l o soko
"The blacker the berry is, the sweeter its juice" (A comment on someone's physical complexion, olive (*melaxni*) skin being a sign of beauty. This traditional attitude is sadly beginning to change, partly due to ideas about 'whiteness' being so central to modern racism but also because of the emphasis on fair skin in advertising and mainstream ideas of beauty).

O manuš o lačho and'o čorripe kerel mandjin, thaj o dilo daži and'e khangeri mardjol
"A good man can find treasure in poverty, while the fool will perish even in church" (We make our own luck, by living according to *Rromanipen*).

Na le tu but pala tj'e punrre, le tu pala tj'e godja
"Don't rely on your feet, rely on your mind" (Use your wits to get out of a situation, you might be able to benefit from it a second time. Run away and you won't get another chance).

Patjival o manuš an'la vi anda gav xaljardo
"A righteous man will profit even in a poor town" (We make our own luck).

O čorro rodel čoripe, ke našavel peski baxt vov korkorro
"The poor man seeks out poverty, because he makes his own luck" (We make our own luck, and failures find other failures to be with).

So či del o berš, del o časo
"What a year may not bring, an hour might" (We never know when something wished for could materialize, it is all up to fate).

And'e čhib naj kokalo
"There are no bones in the tongue" (Yet the tongue can speak hard words).

Tehara brišind dela, numa e balval šukjarela
"The rain may come tomorrow, but the wind will dry it" (Behind every cloud is a silver lining).

Na dža butivar gusto, ka-xasares tj'o skamin
"Don't be a guest too often or you'll lose your seat (at the table)" (Don't overstay your welcome).

O džukel kaj piravel arakhel kokalo
"A dog that wanders will find a bone" (Take some initiative).

Te kheles ekhe rikonesa desa but, čharrela tut and'o muj
"If you play with a puppy too much, it will lick your mouth" (Familiarity breeds contempt).

Makh či hurjal ande muj phanglo
"A fly won't fly into a mouth that's shut" (Keep your mouth shut and you won't get into trouble).

Purani jaska strazo phabjol
"Old firewood catches alight quickly" (Old friendships are easily rekindled).

Cikne čhavorre, cine bede; bare čhavorre, bare bede
"Small children, small troubles, big children, big troubles" (Rich people have problems and worries just like poor people).

E balval či prindžarel kasko vurdon phurdel voj tele
"The wind doesn't recognise whose waggon it blows over" (Misfortunes affect everyone regardless of their wealth or status).

Love and'o vast, bori p'o grast
"Money in the hand and a daughter-in-law on the horse" (The best of all worlds).

Kon del tut o naj ka-del tut o vast
"(He) who gives you a finger will give you a whole hand" (Someone who has given once will give even more a second time).

Rode tj'a borja e kanensa, nič' e jakhensa
"Look for a daughter-in-law with your ears, not with your eyes" (Learn about her reputation, don't be persuaded only by her beauty).

And'o bidžuklesko gav phirel o birovljako Rrom
"Only in the village with no dogs will walk the man with no stick" (There are no villages without any dogs, so always carry a stick. Be prepared).

Khanči či cirdel sumunci sar bidandengi čhirikli
"Nothing succeeds like a toothless bird" (It is natural that you will succeed, since all birds are toothless).

Na xanrrunde kaj či xal tut
"Don't scratch where you don't itch" (Don't make trouble. Let sleeping dogs lie).

O korro kaj phenel ke čhudela barr pe tute, lesko punrro musaj vuže t'azbal barr
"The blind man who threatens to stone you, his foot must already be touching a stone" (If someone has made a threat, he must be confident that he can carry it out; be careful).

Gadžo čorel grastes, Rrom čorel petalo
"The non-Romani steals a horse, the Romani steals a horseshoe" (like the differences in society, Romani theft is correspondingly minor when compared with non-Romani theft).

Rrom čorel khajnja, gadžo čorel farma
"The Romani steals a chicken, the non-Romani steals the farm" (variant of the above).

Samples of the language: a joke

Ekh Rrom sas kaj čokajilas petalo p'e kovanica ande pesko raxciri. Sar pirosardas les, lolo strefjalas.

Atunči nakhlo gadžo kaj terdilo-pe paša leste. "Čuda" phendas; "Naj desa tato kodo petalo te keres butji lesa? Sar šaj rrevdis?"

"Na, grofone, vušoro šaj rrevdiv o tatipe; ašun – te des ma biš teljarja, čarrava les".

O gadžo anzardja lesk' e love. O Rrom ankerdjas o lil and'o vast, čarradas les, thaj thodja les and'e poseči.

"There was a Rom who was hammering a horseshoe on the anvil in his blacksmith shop. As it grew hot it glowed red.

Then a man passed by, and stopped near to him. 'Goodness', he said, 'Isn't that horseshoe far too hot for you to work with? How can you stand (the heat)?'.

'Oh no, squire, I can easily stand the heat. Listen, if you give me twenty dollars, I'll lick it'. The man passed him the money. The Rom held the note in his hand, licked it, and put it in his pocket".

Questions

1   It is frequently said that Romani is a 'poor' language, and sometimes it has even been said that it is not a proper language at all, but a jargon. Why – and is it true?
2   It is frequently said that Romani is not a written language. Why – and is it true?
3   When and how do languages get new words? Give five examples from your own language.
4   How do proverbs reflect the Romani worldview? What is their purpose?
5   Why is creating a common written dialect of Romani such a difficult job?

Romani grammar

O ne of the most interesting characteristics of Romani is that it has two sets of grammatical rules: one for its Asian component, called *thematic*, and one for its European component, called *athematic*. The thematic rules apply to all the words from languages up to and including Byzantine Greek; the athematic rules apply, broadly speaking, to everything acquired from Balkan Greek onwards. The grammar for the thematic component is mainly Indian, and very regular, while the grammar for the athematic part of the language is more complex. For this reason, it isn't entirely accurate to call Romani a wholly Indian language; it seems to have finished taking shape only during the period of its contact with Greek, and so has a 'Balkan' character as well.

Thematic vocabulary is common to all Romani dialects, and it is the athematic loanwords from other languages that make one dialect different from another. As a dialect loses more and more of its original thematic vocabulary and replaces it with foreign adoptions, so it becomes less and less easily understood by speakers of other dialects. A short summary of Vlax is provided here, and the proverbs and text in the preceeding chapter demonstrate its grammar at work. For a more detailed description of the language, see Hancock (1995) and Matras (2002).

Romani has two pronoun cases (subject and oblique) and three noun cases (subject, oblique and vocative); it also has two genders (masculine and feminine) and two numbers (singular and plural). Adjectives and articles (the words for "the" and "a") that accompany nouns must take the appropriate case, gender and number endings to match them. The following sentences illustrate their regular thematic and athematic endings:

1. Articles, adjective and nouns.

Thematic:

(a) singular masculine subject, singular feminine oblique (object)
"the young boy sees the old girl"
o tern-*o* rakl-*o* dikh-*el la* phur-*ja* rakl-*ja*
(b) plural masculine subject, plural feminine oblique
"the young boys see the old girls"
le tern-*e* rakl-*e* dikh-*en le* phur-*e* rakl-*jan*
(c) singular feminine subject, singular masculine oblique
"the old girl sees the young boy"
e phur-*i* rakl-*i* dikh-*el le* phur-*e* rakl-*es*
(d) plural feminine subject, plural masculine oblique
"the old girls see the young boys"
le phur-*e* rakl-*ja* dikh-*en le* pur-*e* rakl-*en*

Athematic:

(a) singular masculine subject, singular feminine oblique
"the bald banker befriends the happy customer"
     o pljac-*o* bankožir-*o* brot-*il la* vesol-*onja* khastomank-*à*
(b) plural masculine subject, plural feminine oblique
"the bald bankers befriend the happy customers"
     le pljac-*i* bankožir-*ulja* brot-*in le* vesol-*one* khastomànč-*jan*
(c) singular feminine subject, singular masculine oblique
    "the happy customer befriends the bald banker"
     e vesol-*o* khastomànk-*a* brot-*il le* pljac-*one* bankožir-*os*
(d) plural feminine subject, plural masculine oblique
    "the happy customers befriend the bald bankers"
     le vesol-*i* khastomànč-*i* brot-*in le* pljac-*one* bankožir-*on*

2. The vocative case.

This is the form of the noun used in direct address; mostly it is used with personal names, thus

   "Here are Steve and Nasta"
    Ake o Stev-*o* thaj e Nast-*a*

"Hey, Steve! Hey, Nasta!"
    Stev-**ane**! Nast-**o**!
Also
   " Men; boys; God; beautiful flower"
        Rrom(-**a**); čhav-**e**; o De(ve)l; šukar luludj-**i**
   "Men!; boys!; oh God; oh beautiful flower!"
        Rrom-**ale**!; čhav-**ale**!; Devl-**a**; joj šukar-**e** luludj-**ijo**!

3. Pronouns.

The personal pronouns have the following forms; note that *Tu* and *Tume* have capital initial letters:

Singular subject		*Singular oblique*	
"I"	**me**	"Me"	**man**
"You"	**Tu**	"You"	**Tut**
"He"	**vov**	"Him"	**les**
"She"	**voj**	"Her"	**la**
		"Himself"	**pes**
		"Herself"	**pes**

Plural subject		*Plural oblique*	
"We"	**ame**	"Us"	**amen**
"You"	**Tume**	"You"	**Tumen**
"They"	**von**	"Them"	**len**
		"Themselves"	**pen**

4. Postpositions

Four different postpositions may be added to the oblique forms of the nouns and pronouns (the first (-*sa*) loses its *s* following another *s*). These are

-**sa** "with"
-**te** "at"
-**tar** "from: by"
-**ke** "to; for"

The last three become -**de**, -**dar** and -**ge** when they follow the final -*n* of the plural oblique:

> "the boy (oblique); from the boy; for the boy; with the boy; at the boy"
>> le rakl-*es*; le rakl-*es-tar*; le rakl-*es-ke*; le rakl-*es-sa*; le rakl-*es-te*
>
> "me; from me; for me; with me; at me"
>> man; man-*dar*; man-*ge*; man-*sa*; man-*de*

Together with *si* ("there is", there are"), the "at" (-*te*/-*de*) postposition is used to express "have", thus *si le rakleste mobili* "the boy has a car", lit. "there is at the boy a car".

5. The possessive endings

Possessive nouns and pronouns are like adjectives, and take the same endings. To make a possessive noun, a -**k**- (or a -**g**- after the plural -**n**) is added to the oblique case, and then followed by the appropriate gender, number and case ending as in (1) above:

le raklesk-*o* gad
  "the boy's shirt"
le raklesk-*i* stadji
  "the boy's hat"
le raklesk-*e* gada
  "the boy's shirts"
le raklesk-*e* stadja
  "the boy's hats

la rakljak-*o* gad
  "the girl's blouse"
la rakljak-*i* stadji
  "the girl's hat"
la rakljak-*e* gada
  "the girl's blouses"
la rakljak-*e* stadja
  "the girl's hats"
murr-*o* gad

le rakleng-*o* gad
  "the boys' shirt"
le rakleng-*i* stadji
  "the boys' hat"
le rakleng-*e* gada
  "the boys' shirts"
le rakleng-*e* stadja
  "the boys' hats"

le rakljang-*o* gad
  "the girls' blouse"
le rakljang-*i* stadji
  "the girls' hat"
le rakljang-*e* gada
  "the girls' blouses"
le rakljang-*e* stadja
  "the girls' hats"
  "my shirt"

murr-*i* stadji	"my hat"
murr-*e* stadja	"my hats"
Tjir-*o* gad	"your shirt"
Tjir-*i* stadji	"your hat"
Tjir-*e* stadja	"your hats"
lesk-*o* gad	"his shirt"
lesk-*i* stadji	"his hat"
lesk-*e* stadja	"his hats"
lak-*o* gad	"her blouse"
lak-*i* stadji	"her hat"
lak-*e* stadja	"her hats"
pesk-*o* gad	"his, her own shirt"
pesk-*i* stadji	"his, her own hat"
pesk-*e* stadja	"his, her own hats"
amar-*o* gad	"our shirt"
amar-*i* stadji	"our hat"
amar-*e* stadja	"our hats"
Tumar-*o* gad	"your shirt"
Tumar-*i* stadji	"your hat"
Tumar-*e* stadja	"your hats"
leng-*o* gad	"their shirt"
leng-*i* stadji	"their hat"
leng-*e* stadja	"their hats"
peng-*o* gad	"their own shirt"
peng-*i* stadji	"their own hat"
peng-*e* stadja	"their own hats"

Nouns can be made from other parts of speech using a number of endings. The thematic ending -*pe(n)* goes with feminine adjectives, e.g. *sasti* "healthy", *sastipe*, *sastipen* "health" or -*be(n)*, which goes with verbs, e.g. *xa-* "eat", *xabe*, *xaben* "food". The athematic ending is -*mos*: *mar-i-* "to make dirty", *marimos* "dirtiness, pollution". The plural for both the thematic and the athematic endings in Vlax is -*mata* (*xa(j)mata*, *mari-mata*), though other dialects pluralise -*pe(n)* and -*be(n)* as -*p(e)na* and -*b(e)na*. The distinction between the thematic and athematic endings, and between those which go with adjectives and those which go with nouns, is not regularly maintained any more.

6. Adverbs.

Thematic and athematic adverbs also take different endings.

Thematic:
   "they are walking slowly"
   lokorr-*es* pirav-*en* (< *lokorro* "slow")
Athematic:
   "they are walking quickly"
   fug-*ones* pirav-*en* (< *fugo* "fast")

7. Verbs.

These have two basic tenses, the present and simple past, or aorist, from which two more tenses (the perfect and the pluperfect) can be made by adding the suffix -*as*. There are also some other extended verb forms such as the passive, examples of which are given below. There is no infinitive in Vlax ('*to run*', '*to jump*', etc.); its equivalent is expressed with *te*, thus "I want to go" is *mangav te džav*, lit. "I want that I go".

Thematic verbs

Regular thematic verbs are built up from a stem or root, which may end in a consonant or an -*a*, to which the following endings are added in the present tense:

rov- "cry"		*asa*- "laugh"	
me rov-*av*	"I am crying"	me asa-*v*	"I am laughing"
Tu rov-*es*	"you are crying"	Tu asa-*s*	"you are laughing"
vov rov-*el*	"he is crying"	vov asa-*l*	"he is laughing"
voj rov-*el*	"she is crying"	voj asa-*l*	"she is laughing"
ame rov-*as*	"we are crying"	ame asa-*s*	"we are laughing"
Tume rov-*en*	"you are crying"	Tume asa-*n*	"you are laughing"
von rov-*en*	"they are crying"	von asa-*n*	"they are laughing"

The simple past tense is made by adding a -*d*- or an -*l*- to the verb stem, (-*d*- after those ending in -*b*, -*čh*, -*g*, -*k(h)*, -*m*, -*ng*, -*p(h)*, -*s*, -*š*, -*t(h)* and -

(d)ž, and *-l-* after stems ending in *-d, -l, -n, -r* and *-rr*), then followed by the appropriate endings:

me phen-***av***	"I say"	me dikh-***av***	"I see"
me phen-***d-em***	"I said"	me dikh-***l-em***	"I saw"
Tu phen-***d-an***	"you said"	Tu dikh-***l-an***	"you saw"
vov phen-***d-as***	"he said"	vov dikh-***l-as***	"he saw"
voj phen-***d-as***	"she said"	voj dikh-***l-as***	"she saw"
ame phen-***d-am***	"we said"	ame dikh-***l-am***	"we saw"
Tume phen-***d-an***	"you said"	Tume dikh-***l-an***	"you saw"
von phen-***d-e***	"they said"	von dikh-***l-e***	"they saw"

By adding *-as* to the present and to the simple past, two more tenses, the imperfect and the pluperfect, are easily made:

me dikh-***av***	"I see; I'm seeing"
me dikh-***av-as***	"I was seeing", *or* "I used to see"
me dikh-***l-em***	"I saw"
me dikh-***l-em-as***	"I had seen"

The future tense is made either by adding an *-a* to the present tense forms, or by placing the word **kam** before them:

me dikh-***av-a***	
or	"I will see"
me **kam**-dikh-***av***	

Athematic verbs

These fall into two sets: those that have an *-i-* following the stem, and those that have an *-o-*; there is no difference otherwise. In the present tense, they behave like *-a-* stem thematic verbs; that is, they only take the consonant endings:

vol-***i-***	"love"	ram-***o-***	"write"
me vol-***i-v***	"I love"	me ram-***o-v***	"I write"
Tu vol-***i-s***	"you love"	Tu ram-***o-s***	"you write"
vov vol-***i-l***	"he loves"	vov ram-***o-l***	"he writes"

voj vol-*i-l*	"she loves"	voj ram-*o-l*	"she writes
ame vol-*i-s*	"we love"	ame ram-*o-s*	"we write"
Tume vol-*i-n*	"you love"	Tume ram-*o-n*	"you write"
von vol-*i-n*	"they love"	von ram-*o-n*	"they write"

The simple past is regularly made by adding -*sar-d-* to the stem, followed by the relevant endings:

me vol-*i-sar-d-em*	"I loved": *me volisardem la* "I loved her"
me ram-*o-sar-d-em*	"I wrote": *me ramosardem lake* "I wrote to her"
Tu vol-*i-sar-d-an*	"you loved": *Tu volisardan les* "you loved him"
Tu ram-*o-sar-d-an*	"you wrote": *Tu ramosardan mange* "you wrote to me"

The passive

The passive translates e.g. "I was made"(which also means "I was born") rather than "I made", or "he is hidden" rather than "he hides". With thematic verbs, the present passive is made by following the simple past stem with -**jo**- and then the present tense endings. The simple past passive is the simple past stem plus -**il**- plus the past tense endings (but with -**o**/-**i** for the third persons):

Present		*Past*	
me ker-*d-jo-v*	"I am made"	me ker-*d-il-em*	"I was made"
Tu ker-*d-jo-s*	"you are made"	Tu ker-*d-il-an*	"you were made"
vov ker-*d-jo-l*	"he is made"	vov ker-*d-il-o*	"he was made"
voj ker-*d-jo-l*	"she is made"	voj ker-*d-il-i*	"she was made"

With athematic verbs, the endings are as follows, with *farb-o-* "paint":

Present	*Past*
me farb-*o-v*	me farb-*o-sar-d-em*
"I paint"	"I painted"
me farb-*o-sav-av*	me farb-*o-sa'-il-em*
"I am painted"	"I was painted"

Tu farb-*o-sav-es*   Tu farb-*o-sa'-il-an*
"you are painted"   "you were painted"
vov farb-*o-sav-el*   vov farb-*o-sa'-il-o*
"he is painted"   "he was painted"

The causative

Causative verbs are used to show that something has been *caused* to
happen, for example "I cause to fall" would express "I drop", "you cause
to learn" would express "you teach". They can be created from verbs,
nouns or adjectives. Those made from verbs place -**av**- before the endings in the present tense, and -**a'**-**d**- before the endings in the past tense
(**a'** here, as well as in the past passive above, shows that the -**v**- has been
dropped after the **a**; like the hyphens in these words, it is not written in
conventional spelling).

Present		*Past*	
me per-**av**	"I fall"	me pe-**l**-**em**	"I fell" (irregular, from per-**d**-**em**)
me per-**av**-**av**	"I drop"	me per-**a'**-**d**-**em**	"I dropped"
Tu per-**av**-**es**	"you drop"	Tu per-**a'**-**d**-**an**	"you dropped"
vov per-**av**-**el**	"he drops"	vov per-**a'**-**d**-**as**	"he dropped"
voj per-**av**-**el**	"she drops"	voj per-**a'**-**d**-**as**	"she dropped"

Causatives derived from both adjectives and nouns put -**jar**- directly after
the stem and before the endings:

With an adjective

tang	"narrow"
tang-jar-	"make narrow; cause to be narrow"
me tang-jar-av les	"I'm making it narrow"
me tang-jar-d-em les	"I made it narrow"

With a noun

xoli	"anger"
xol-jar-	"make angry; cause to be angry"
xol-jar-av le dženen	"I'm making the people angry"
xol-jar-d-em le dženen	"I made the people angry"

The inchoative

This is a very common kind of verb in Vlax Romani. *Inchoative* means something like "becoming", and all of these verbs are derived from adjectives; for example from the adjective "red" the verb "to become red" or "to redden" can easily be made. The endings are exactly the same as those used to create passive verbs. From *thulo* "fat", are:

Present		*Past*	
me thul-*jo-v*	"I grow fat"	me thul-*il-em*	"I grew fat"
Tu thul-*jo-s*	"you grow fat"	Tu thul-*il-an*	"you grew fat"
vov thul-*jo-l*	"he grows fat"	vov thul-*il-o*	"he grew fat"
voj thul-*jo-l*	"she grows fat"	voj thul-*il-i*	"she grew fat"

Compare this inchoative meaning with the causative meaning of "to cause (something) to be fat" (*vov thuljarel le bales thaj o balo thuljol* "he's fattening up the pig and the pig is growing fatter").

The *BE*-verb is as follows:

me sim	"I am"	me simas	"I was"
Tu san	"you are"	Tu sanas	"you were"
vov si	"he is"	vov sas	"he was"
voj si	"she is"	voj sas	"she was"
ame sam	"we are"	ame samas	"we were"
Tume san	"you are"	Tume sanas	"you were"
von si	"they are"	von sas	"they were"

Participles

The present participle is the stem plus -*indoj*: *dikh-indoj* "seeing".

The past participle for thematic verbs is the simple past stem with -*o* (masculine), -*i* (feminine) or -*e* (plural): *dikh-l-o* "seen", *phager-d-i* "broken", *beš-l-e* "seated".

The past participle for athematic verbs is the present stem with the -*i*- or -*o*-, followed by -*me* (from Greek): *vol-i-me* "beloved", *ram-o-me* "written".

The word *či* before the verb makes it negative:

me či volisardem la	"I didn't love her"
me či ramosardem lake	"I didn't write to her"
Tu či volisardan les	"you didn't love him"
Tu či ramosardan mange	"you didn't write to me"

The third person of the *BE*-verb has its own negatives: **naj** in the present and **nas** in the past:

murro amal si	"he's my friend"
naj murro amal	"he isn't my friend"
murro amal sas	"he was my friend"
nas murre amala	"they weren't my friends"

Recommended sources

Standards in Romani Studies

The popular perception of Romanies sometimes manifests itself in the poor quality of the scholarship associated with them; it seems to be assumed that less academic rigour is necessary in this field than would be demanded in other areas. Doctorates have been awarded to graduate students whose dissertations were supervised by committees whose members had no expertise whatsoever in Romani Studies. Since 1997 at least three "Gypsy" courses have been established at different American universities by faculty members who have no qualifications in the area, and who have never met any Romanies, and whose list of readings contain unacademic and misleading titles; one such course description dated 2001 may be viewed at:

http://athena.louisville.edu/a-s/english/subcultures/colors/teal/jmjone02/ jonefrontpg.htm

and another is at: *http://polyglot .lss.wisc.edu/slavic/courses/370.html*

The same standards of scholarship must apply to the study of our people as they would to any other human population.

Books and articles about Romanies number in the tens of thousands but practically every single one of them has been written by an outsider and most of those by people who have never actually met any Romanies in their lives. It would be hard to imagine a book about modern-day Bulgarians or Slovaks being taken seriously, if it had been written by someone who had never been to Bulgaria or Slovakia and who had never talked to anyone from those countries. This doesn't mean that those books are all inaccurate or misleading, but it does mean that the teacher or journalist or researcher coming to the topic for the first time has no means of knowing what is reliable and what is not.

This has begun to change in the past few years. With the increased awareness of the Romani presence in Europe and the rest of the world, new and far more reliable publications have appeared, not only by scholars who have interacted with us at first hand, but by our own Romani authors as well. The following list of titles is only a guide to what is available, but they would make a very good start towards building a Romani Studies library. It includes bibliographies (Danbakli, Gronemeyer, Hohmann, Tong), materials on the *Porrajmos* (Fings, Kenrick, Rose), on Romani history (Crowe, Fraser, Liégeois, Vossen), education (by Liégeois), law (Weyrauch), the literary 'gypsy' image (Awosusi, Briel, Dougherty, Green, Hund, Niemandt, Norrell, Tebbutt, Wendler-Funaro, Wright), language (Bakker and Kyuchukov, Boretzky and Igla, Hancock, Matras), politics (Acton, Guy), slavery (Hancock), literature (Tong, Baumann, Hancock, Dowd and Djurić) and identity (Lee, Marushiakova, Heuss et al.).

The University of Hertfordshire Press in Britain specializes in Romani-related titles, several of which are listed here; the website for these is *http://www.herts.ac.uk/UHPress/Gypsies.html*. It is also the English-language publisher for the *Interface Collection*, directed by the Centre de Recherches Tsiganes at René Descartes University, an excellent ongoing series of volumes, now numbering nearly thirty, available from *crt@paris5.sorbonne.fr*. Other sources of up-to-date social and political information published about Romanies are the two series of reports by the European Roma Rights Center in Budapest (*http://errc.org*), and by the Project on Ethnic Relations in Princeton (*http://www.netcom/~ethnic/per.html*). Many academic and other articles from journals are reproduced on the Patrin website at *http://www.geocities/Paris/5121/patrin.htm* and may be printed out from there; links are also found on Patrin to other Romani websites. Current news items concerning Romanies are found every day on the RomNews Network at *http://www.romnews.com*. A useful list of additional websites is found as an appendix to Bakker et al. I have also added one title that, while it only mentions Romanies twice is very useful in helping to explain and understand the social attitudes which mainstream society has towards people perceived to be 'different' (Goffman).

Acton, Thomas, ed, 2000. *Gypsy Politics and Traveller Identity*. Hatfield: University of Hertfordshire Press.

Acton, Thomas, ed, 2000. *Scholarship and the Gypsy Struggle: Commitment in Romani Studies*. Hatfield: University of Hertfordshire Press.

Acton, Thomas, and Gary Mundy, eds, 1997. *Romani Culture and Gypsy Identity*. Hatfield: University of Hertfordshire Press.

Awosusi, Anita, 2000. *Zigeunerbilder in der Kinder- und Jugendliteratur*. Heidelberg: Wunderhorn.

Bakker, **Peter**, and Hristo Kyuchukov, eds, 2000. *What is the Romani Language?* Hatfield: University of Hertfordshire Press. Interface Collection, Vol. 21.

Baumann, Max P, ed, 2000. *Music, Language and Literature of the Roma and Sinti*. Berlin: VWB Verlag.

Boretzky, Norbert, and Birgit Igla, 1994. *Wörterbuch Roman-Deutsch-English für den Südosteuropäischen Raum*. Wiesbaden: Harrassowitz.

Briel, Petra-Gabriele, 1989. *Lumpenkind und Traumprinzessin: Zur Sozialgestalt der Zigeuner in der kinder- und Jugendliteratur seit dem 19. Jahrhundert*. Giessen: Focus Verlag.

Cortés, Carlos E, 2000. *The Children are Watching: How the Media Teach about Diversity*. New York and London: Teachers' College Press. Especially the Prologue: "It began with the Gypsies", *pp* 1-3.

Crowe, David, 1994. *A History of the Gypsies of Eastern Europe and Russia*. New York: St. Martin's Press.

Danbakli, Marielle, 2001. *Roma, Gypsies: Texts Issued by International Institutions*. Hatfield: University of Hertfordshire Press. Interface Collection, Vol. 5.

Dougherty, Frank T., 1980. *The Gypsies in Western Literature*. Doctoral dissertation, The University of Illinois, Urbana-Champaign.

Fings, Karola, Herbert Heuss and Frank Sparing, 1997. *The Gypses during the Second World War. 1: From 'Race Science' to the Camps*. Hatfield: University of Hertfordshire Press. Interface Collection, Vol. 12.

Fraser, Angus, 1992. *The Gypsies*. Oxford: Blackwell.

Goffman, Erving, 1963. *Stigma: Notes on the Management of Spoiled Identity*. Englewood Cliffs: Prentice-Hall.

Green, Rosalind M., 2001. *Romancing the other: An Exploration of the Fictional Representation and Appropriation of the Gypsy in the English novel between 1850-1930*. Masters thesis, The University of Melbourne.

Gronemeyer, Reimer, 1983. *Zigeuner in Osteuropa: Eine Bibliographie zu den Ländern Polen, Tschechoslowakei und Ungarn*. Munich: K G Saur.

Guy, Will, ed, 2001. *Between Past and Future: The Roma of Central and Eastern Europe*. Hatfield: University of Hertfordshire Press.

Hancock, Ian, 1987. *The Pariah Syndrome*. Ann Arbor: Karoma. This is out of print but is available on the Patrin website: *http://www.geocities.com/Paris/5121/patrin/htm*.

Hancock, Ian, 1995. *A Handbook of Vlax Romani*. Columbus: Slavica.

Hancock, Ian, Siobhan Dowd and Rajko Djurić, eds, 1998. *The Roads of the Roma*. Hatfield: University of Hertfordshire Press.

Hohmann, Joachim S, 1992. *Neue Deutsche Zigeunerbibliographie*. Frankfurt: Peter Lang. Vol. 8 of Lang's Studien zur Ziganologie und Folkloristik series.

Hund, Wulf D., ed, 2000. *Zigeunerbilder: Schnittmuster Rassistischer Ideologie*. Duisberg: DISS.

Kenrick, Donald, 1998. *Historical Dictionary of the Gypsies (Romanies)*. Lanham: The Scarecrow Press.

Kenrick, Donald, ed, 1999. *The Gypsies during the Second World War.* 2: *In the Shadow of the Swastika.* Hatfield: University of Hertfordshire Press. Interface Collection, Vol. 13

Kenrick, Donald, and Grattan Puxon, 1995. *Gypsies Under the Swastika.* Hatfield: University of Hertfordshire Press. Interface Collection, Vol. 8.

Lee, Kenneth, 2002. *Constructing Romani Strangerhood.* Doctoral dissertation, Newcastle University, Newcastle, Australia.

Liégeois, Jean-Pierre, 1988. *Gypsies, an Illustrated History.* London: Al-Saqi Books.

Liégeois, Jean-Pierre, 1998. *School Provision for Ethnic Minorities: The Gypsy Paradigm.* Paris: Centre de Recherches Tsiganes, René Descartes University. Interface Collection, Vol. 11.

Marushiakova, E., Herbert Heuss et al., 2001. *Identity Formation among Minorities in the Balkans: The Cases of Roms, Egyptians and Ashkali in Kosovo.* Sofia: Minority Studies Society.

Matras, Yaron, 2002. *Romani: A Linguistic Introduction.* Cambridge: The University Press.

Mode, Heinz, 1984. *Zigeunermärchen aus Aller Welt.* Leipzig: Insel Verlag. 4 vols.

Niemandt, Hans-Dieter, 1992. *Die Zigeuner in den Romanischen Literaturen.* Frankfurt: Peter Lang. Vol. 6 of Lang's *Studien zur Ziganologie und Folkloristik* series.

Norrell, Elisabeth Renée van Tuyll, 1981. *Le Rôle des Bohémiens dans la Littérature Française du Dix-Neuvième Siècle.* Doctoral dissertation, The University of Alabama.

Ortmeyer, Christoph, Elke Peters and Daniel Strauss, 1998. *Antiziganismus: Geschichte und Gegenwart Deutscher Sinti und Roma.* Wiesbaden: Hessisches Landesinstitut für Pädagogik.

Rose, Romani, ed, 1999. *Den Rauch Hatten Wir Täglich vor Augen: Der Nationalsozialistische Völkermord an den Sinti und Roma.* Heidelberg: Wunderhorn.

Szente, Veronika, 2001. *Racial Discrimination and Violence Against Roma in Europe.* Budapest: European Roma Rights Centre. Statement submitted to the UN Committee on the Elimination of Racial Discrimination.

Tebbutt, Susan, ed, 1998. *Sinti und Roma: Gypsies in German-speaking Society and Literature.* New York and Oxford: Berghahn Books.

Tong, Diane, 1989. *Gypsy Folktales.* New York: Harcourt Brace Jovanovich.

Tong, Diane, 1995. *Gypsies: A Multidisciplinary Annotated Bibliography.* New York and London: Garland Publishers.

Tong, Diane, ed, 1998. *Gypsies: An Interdisciplinary Reader.* New York and London: Garland Publishing.

Vossen, Rüdiger, 1983. *Zigeuner: Roma, Sinti, Gitanos, Gypsies Zwischen Verfolgung und Romantisierung.* Frankfurt: Ullstein.

Wendler-Funaro, Carl de, 1958. *The Gitano in Spanish Literature.* Doctoral dissertation, Columbia University, New York.

Weyrauch, Walter, ed, 2001. *Gypsy Law: Romani Legal Traditions and Culture.* Berkeley and London: University of California Press.

Wright, Rosemary, 1994. *The Representation of the Romani/Gypsy in 19th and 20th Century Writings.* Bachelor of Arts thesis, University of technology, Sydney.

Works referenced in text

Acton, Thomas A., 1974. *Gypsy Politics and Social Change*. London: Routledge and Kegan Paul.

Acton, Thomas, and Ilona Klímová, 2001. "The International Romani Union: An east European answer to west European questions?", *in* Guy, 2001:157–219.

Alecsandri, Vasile, 1844. *Istoria unui Galban*. Bucharest.

Altinoz, Ismael, 2001. "Los gitanos en la sociedad otomana". *Nevipens Romani*, 306:4.

Anderson, Gwen and Bridget Tighe, 1973. "Gypsy culture and health care", *American Journal of Nursing*, 73(2):282–5.

Anon., 1856. "The Gipsies of the Danube." *Chambers's Journal of Popular Literature*, 122:273–275.

Anon., 1990. "Plans shelved for Gypsy site", *The Surrey Advertiser*, 25 May, p. 1.

Baloch, Aziz, 1968. *Spanish Cante Jondo and its Origin in Sindhi Music*. Hyderabad: The Mehran Arts Council.

Bartels, Erik and Gudrun Brun, 1943. *The Gipsies in Denmark*. Copenhagen: Munksgaard.

Bauer, Yehuda, 1994. "Gypsies", *in* Gutman and Berenbaum, 1994:441–455.

BBC, 2001. "Europe's neglected race: European Roma face discrimination". Internet news bulletin for 5 September 2001, British Broadcasting Corporation World Service.

Beck, Sam, 1985. "The Rumanian Gypsy problem", *in* J Grumet (ed), *Papers from the Fourth and Fifth Annual Meetings of the Gypsy Lore Society, North American Chapter, New York*: GLS(NAC) Monograph No. 2, pp 100–109.

Behrendt, Johannes, 1939. "Die Wahrheit über die Zigeuner", *NS-Partei Korrespondenz*, 10, No. 3.

Bhalla, Vijender, 1992. "Ethnicity and Indian origins of Gypsies of Eastern Europe and the USSR: A bio-anthropological perspective", *in* K S Singh, ed, *Ethnicity, Caste and People*. Moscow and Delhi, pp 323–346.

Bhattacharya, Deben, 1965. *The Gypsies*. London: Record Books.

Binding, Karl, and Alfred Hoche, 1920. *Die Freigabe der Vernichtung Lebensunwerten Lebens*. Leipzig: Felix Meiner.

Block, Martin, 1936. *Zigeuner: Ihre Leben und ihre Seele*. Leipzig: Bibliographisches Institut AG.

Breitman, Richard, 1991. *The Architect of Genocide: Himmler and the Final Solution*. Hanover and London: University Press of New England.

Broad, Percy, 1966. "KZ Auschwitz: Erinnerungen eines SS Mannes". *Hefte von Auschwitz*, 9:7–48.

Burleigh, Michael, and Wolfgang Wippermann, 1991. *The Racial State: Germany, 1933–1945*. Cambridge: The University Press.

Büsching, Johann Gustav, 1810. *Pantheon*. Leipzig and Nenden.

Chamberlain, Houston S, 1899. *Die Grundlagen des Neunzehnten Jahrhunderts*. Leipzig.

Colson, Félix, 1839. *De l'Etat Présent et de l'Avenir des Principauts de Moldavie et de Valachie*. Paris.

Cook, Christopher, ed, 2002. *Pears Cyclopedia 2001–2002*. London: Penguin Books.

Crabb, James, 1832. *The Gipsies' Advocate*. London: Nisbet, Westley and Co.

Cribb, Billy, 2001. *Tarmac Warrior*. Edinburgh and London: Mainstream Publishing.

Darwin, Charles, 1871. *Die Abstammung des Menschen und die Geschlichtiche Zuchtwahl*. Stuttgart: Schweitzerbartsche Verlag.

Davidson, Thomas, 1890. "Mr. Groome's theory of the diffusion of folk-tales by means of the Gypsies," *Journal of the Gypsy Lore Society*, 2:113–5.

De Peyster, J Watts, 1887. *Gypsies: Some Curious Investigations*. Edinburgh: Aungerville.

Dillmann, Alfred, 1905. *Zigeuner-Buch*. Munich: Wildsche.

Di Renzo, R, ed, 2001. *Gypsies*. Special issue of *Colours*, No. 42. Cattena: Benetton Group SpA.

Dunstan, G R, 1965. "A note on an early ingredient of racial prejudice in Western Europe", *Race*, 6(4):334–9.

Elkind, Deborah, 2000. "Apache à go-go", *Alice Magazine*, 2000(1):1.

ERRC, 2001. *European Roma Rights Centre: Biannual Report 1999–2000*. Budapest: The European Roma Rights Centre.

Fonseca, Isabel, 1996. *Bury Me Standing: The Gypsies and their Journey*. New York: Random House.

Foster, Ellsworth D, and James Laughlin Hughes, eds, 1924. *The American Educator: A New and Thoroughly Modern Reference Work Designed to Meet the Needs of Every Age*. Chicago: Ralph Durham and Co.

Fraser, Angus, 1989. "Looking into the seeds of time." Paper read at the Annual Meeting of the Gypsy Lore Society, Toronto, 7–9April 1989.

Glase, Robert S., 1998. *Gypsies (Romanies) of the Sixteenth Century Ottoman Empire*. Seminar Report: Portland State University.

Godwin, Peter, 2001. "Gypsies: the Outsiders," *National Geographic*, 199(4):72–101.

Grellmann, Heinrich M, 1783. *Die Zigeuner. Ein historische Versuch über die Lebensart und Verfaßung*. Dessau and Leipzig. English edition 1807.

Gresham, David, et al., 2001. "Origins and divergence of the Roma", *American Journal of Human Genetics*, 69:1314–1331.

Groome, Francis H, 1899. *Gypsy Folk Tales*. London: Hurst and Blackett.

Gutman, Israel, and Michael Berenbaum, eds, 1994. *Anatomy of the Auschwitz Death Camp*. Bloomington: Indiana University Press.

Guy, Will, ed, 2001. *Between Past and Future: The Roma of Central and Eastern Europe*. Hatfield: University of Hertfordshire Press.

Haberer, Eric, 2001. "The second sweep: Gendarmerie killings of Jews and Gypsies on January 29th, 1942", *Journal of Genocide Research*, 3(2):207–18.

Hancock, Ian, 1987. *The Pariah Syndrome*. Ann Arbor: Karoma.

Hancock, Ian, 1992. "The roots of inequity: Romani cultural rights in their historical and social context", *Immigrants and Minorities*, 11(1):1–20.

Harriott, John S., 1830. "Observations on the Oriental origin of the Romanichal, or tribe miscalled Gypsey and Bohemian", *Transactions of the Royal Asiatic Society*, 2:518–558.

Haşdeu, Bogdan P., 1865, *Razvan şi Vidra*. Bucharest.

Heine, Marie-Agnes, 2001. *Roma Victims of the Nazi Regime May Be Entitled to Compensation*. Geneva: International Organization for Migration, Office of Public Information.

Heye, Uwe-Karsten, Joachim Sartorius and Ulrich Bopp, eds, 2000. *Learning from History: The Nazi Era and the Holocaust in German Education*. Berlin: Press and Information Office of the Federal Government.

Hoffman, Joseph, 1988. "Gypsy-Jewish music goes home", *The Jerusalem Post*, September 24, p.5.

Hübschmannová, Milena, 1972. "What can sociology suggest about the sociology of the Roms?", *Archiv Orientální*, 40:41–64.

Hübschmannová, Milena, 1978. "Jste z rodu antilop, pane Mirgo", *Nový Orient*, 33(9):276–8.

Jayat, Sandra, 1974. *La Longue Route d'une Zingarina*. Paris: Bordas.

Jørstad, Unn, 1972. "Norway's Gypsy minority", *American Scandinavian Review*, 58(2):129–137.

Joshi, A, 1981. "Romani as a mediaeval Aryan language", *Roma*, 6(1):37–9.

Kalaydjieva, Luba, David Gresham and Fransesc Calafell, 1999. *Genetics of the Roma (Gypsies)*. Human Genome Project Special Report. Perth: Centre for Human Genetics, Edith Cowan University.

Kenedi Janos,1966. "Why is the Gypsy the scapegoat and not the Jew?", *East European Reporter* 2(1):11–14.

Kenrick, Donald, and Grattan Puxon, 1972. *The Destiny of Europe's Gypsies*. London: Heinemann.

Kephart, William M, 1982. *Extraordinary Groups*. New York: St. Martin's Press.

Kerim, Usin, 1955. *Gilja la Cehratar*. Sofia: Sumen.

Kishwar, Madhu, 1998. "Naíve outpourings of a self-hating Indian", *Manushi*, 109:3–14. New Delhi.

Kochanowski, Vania de Gila, 1963. *Gypsy Studies*. Delhi: International Academy of Indian Culture. In two volumes.

Kochanowski, Vania de Gila, 1968. "Black Gypsies, white Gypsies", *Diogenes*, 63:2–47.

Kochanowski, Vania de Gila, 1992. *Romano Atmo: L'Ame Tsigane*. Châteauneuf: Wallâda.

Kochanowski, Vania de Gila, 1994. *Parlons Tsigane: Histoire, Culture et Langue du Peuple Tsigane*. Paris: l'Harmattan.

Kochanowski, Vania de Gila, 1995. "Romane čhave and the problems of their intercontinental communication", *Roma*, 42/43:1–34.

Kochanowski, Vania de Gila, 1996. *Le Roi des Serpents*, Volume I of *Les Romané Chavé par Eux-Mêmes*. Châteauneuf: Wallâda.

König, Ulrich, 1989. *Sinti und Roma unter dem Nationalsozialismus*. Bochum: Brockmeyer Verlag.

Kulemann, Rudolph, 1869. "Die Zigeuner", *Unserer Zeit*, 5(1):843–871.

Kulke, Hermann, and Dietmar Rothermund, 1998. *History of India*. London and New York: Routledge.

Kumar, Palash, 2001. Study examines genetics in India's caste system," *The Nando Times*, July 5, pp 1–3.

Lacková, Elena, 1999. *A False Dawn: My Life as a Gypsy Woman in Slovakia*. Hatfield: University of Hertfordshire Press.

Lal, Chaman, 1962. *Gypsies: Forgotten Children of India*. Delhi: Ministry of Information and Broadcasting.

Latham, Judith, 1995. *First US Conference on Gypsies in the Holocaust*. Current Affairs Bulletin No. 3–23928. Washington: Voice of America.

Leblon, Bernard, 2002. *Gypsies and Flamenco*. Second Edition. Hatfield: The University of Hertfordshire Press. Interface Collection, Vol. 6.

Ledgard, Jonathan, 2001. "Europe's spectral nation", *The Economist*, 12 May, 29–31.

Lee, Ken, 2002. "Belated travelling theory, contemporaneous wild praxis: A Romani perspective on the politics of the open end", *in* N Saul and S Tebbutt, eds, *Images and self-images of Romanies/"Gypsies" in European Cultures*. Liverpool: The University Press.

Lee, Ronald, 2001. *The Gypsy Invasion of Canada*. Toronto: Privately-circulated monograph.

Lewy, Guenther, 2000. *The Nazi Persecution of the Gypsies*. Cambridge: The University Press.

Liebich, Richard, 1863. *Die Zigeuner in ihrem Wesen und ihre Sprache*. Leipzig: Brockhaus.

Liégeois, Jean-Pierre, 1976. *Mutation Tsigane: La Révolution Bohémienne*. Paris: Presses Universitaires de France. Editions Complexe.

Lípa, Jiřĭ, 1983. "Priorities in Romani studies", *Newsletter of the North American Chapter of the Gypsy Lore Society*, 6(1):3–4.

Lombroso, Cesare, 1918. *Crime: Its Causes and Remedies*. Boston: Little, Brown and Co.

Marsden, William, 1785. "Observations on the language of the people commonly called Gypsies", *Archæologia*, 7:382–386.

Marushiakova, Elena, and Vesselin Popov, 1997. "The Romanies in the Balkans during the Ottoman Empire", *Roma*, 47:63–72.

Mason, P, 1968. "But oh!, my soul is white", *Encounter*, April, pp 57–61.

Mastana, Sarabjit, and Surinda S Papiha, 1992. "Origin of the Romani Gypsies: genetic evidence", *Zeitschrift für Morphologie und Anthropologie*, 79(1):43–51.

Matras, Yaron, ed, 1998. *The Romani Element in Non-Standard Speech*. Wiesbaden: Harrassowitz.

Maximoff, Matéo, 1946. *Les Ursitory*. Paris: Flammarion.

Maximoff, Matéo, 1955. *Le Prix de la Liberté*. Paris: Flammarion.

Maximoff, Matéo, 1984. *Condamné à Survivre*. Paris: Librairie Chrétienne.

Maximoff, Matéo, 1982. *La Septième Fille*. Romainville: Chez l'Auteur.

Maximoff, Matéo, 1986. *Savina*. Romainville: Wallâda.

Maximoff, Matéo, 1987. *Vinguerka*. Romainville: Chez l'Auteur.

Mayall, David, 1988. *Gypsy-Travellers in Nineteenth-Century Society*. Cambridge: The University Press.

Meyers, Anat E., 1987. *The Gypsy as Child Stealer: Stereotype in American Folklore*. Masters thesis, Department of Folklore, The University of California at Berkeley.

Milton, Sybil, 1992. "Nazi policies towards Roma and Sinti 1933–1945", *Journal of the Gypsy Lore Society*; Fifth series, 2(1):1–18.

Mirga, Andrzej and Nicolae Gheorghe, 1997. *The Roma in the Twenty-First Century: A Policy Paper*. Princeton: The Project on Ethnic Relations.

Moraes, Mello de, 1886. *Os Ciganos no Brasil*. Rio de Janeiro.

Müller-Hill, Benno, 1988. *Murderous Science: Elimination by Scientific Selection of Jews, Gypsies and Others, 1933–1945*. Oxford: The University Press.

Naik, Ranjit, 1978. *Banjara from Barothan*. Report issued at the Second World Romani Congress, Geneva, April 8–11.

Nemeth, David, 2002. *The Gypsy-American: An Ethnographic Study*. Lewiston: The Edwin Mellen Press.

Norton, John, 1927. "Gypsies", *The Sydney Truth*, May 22, p. 1.

Novitch, Miriam, 1968. *Le Genocide des Tziganes Sous le Régime Nazi*. Paris: AMIF and the Ghetto Fighters' House, Israel.

Okely, Judith, 1983. *The Traveller-Gypsies*. Cambridge: The University Press.

Pott, Augustus, 1844. *Die Zigeuner in Europa und Asien*. Halle: Heynemann Verlag.

Proester, Emil, 1940. Vraždění. *Cikánů v Buchenwaldu*. Document No. ÚSv ČSPB–K–135 of the Archives of the Fighters Against Fascism, Prague.

Rakelmann, G A, ed, 1979. *Loseblattsammlung für Unterrich und Bildungsarbeit*. Freiburg im Breisgau.

Raphael, Frederic, 1977. *The Glittering Prizes*. New York: St. Martin's Press.

Rathore, B Shyamala Devi, 1998. "Gypsy music", paper submitted to the Romani Studies conference, Greenwich University, London, 11 June.

Rishi, Weer R, 1976. *Roma: the Punjabi Emigrants in Europe, Central and Middle Asia, the USSR and the Americas*. Patalia: The Patalia Press.

Rishi, Weer R, 1977. "Roma preserve Hindu mythology", *Roma*, 3(1):1–14.

Roleine, Roberte, 1978. *Le Prince d'une Été*. Paris: Tallandier.

Rüdiger, Jacob, 1782–1793. *Neuster Zuwachs der Teutschen Fremden und Allgemeinen Sprachkunde in Eigenen Aufsätzen, Bücheranzeigen und Nachrichten*. Leipzig. In five volumes.

Saint John, Bayle, 1853. "The Gypsy slaves of Wallachia", *Household Words*, 185:139–142.

Salloway, Jeffrey C, 1973. "Medical care utilization among urban Gypsies", *Urban Anthropology*, 2(1):113–126.

Salunke, N B, 1989. "The Rajput Lohars," *Roma*, 30:21–31.

Sampson, John, 1923. "On the origin and early migration of the Gypsies", *Journal of the Gypsy Lore Society*, third series, 2(4):156–169.

Sampson, John, 1926. *The Dialect of the Gypsies of Wales*. Oxford: The Clarendon Press.

Sareen, K N, 1976. "The role of biochemical genetics in tracing the origin of a human group", *Roma*, 2(1):41–5.

Sárosi Bálint, 1970. *Gypsy Music*. Budapest: Corvina Press.

Serboianu, C J Popp, 1930. *Les Tsiganes*. Paris: Payot.

Sharma, S K, 1976. "Roma have ethnic and linguistic connections with India," *Roma*, 2(2):26–30.

Shashi, S S, 1990. *Roma: the Gypsy World*. Delhi: Sandeep Prakashan.

Shields, Audrey, 1993. *Gypsy Stereotypes in Victorian Literature*. Doctoral dissertation, Department of English, New York University, New York.

Shields, Marilyn, 1981. "Selected issues in treating Gypsy patients", *Hospital Physician*, 11:85–92.

Sibley, David, 1981. *Outsiders in Urban Societies*. Oxford: Blackwell.

Simson, Walter, 1865. *A History of the Gipsies*. London: Sampson, Lowe.

Singhal, D P, 1982. *Gypsies: Indians in Exile*. Meerut: Archana Publications.

Siváková, D, 1983. "Estimation of the degree of assimilation of the Gypsy population based on genetic distance calculations", *Anthropologia*, 28–29:95–102.

Soulis, George C, 1961. "Gypsies in the Byzantine Empire and the Balkans in the late Middle Ages", *Dumbarton Oaks Papers*, 15:142–165.

Starkie, Walter, 1972. "Gypsies: the eternal travellers", introduction to the Newcastle reprint of Xavier Petulengro's *A Romany Life* (London: Methuen, 1935), pp *i–iv.*

SMAB (State Museum of Auschwitz-Birkenau), 1993. *Memorial Book: the Gypsies at Auschwitz-Birkenau*. Munich: K.G. Saur.

Stockin, Jimmy, 2000. *On the Cobbles: The Life of a Bare-Knuckle Gypsy Warrior*. Edinburgh and London: Mainstream Publishing.

Thomas, James D, 1985. "Gypsies and American medical care", *Annals of Internal Medicine*, 102(6):842–5.

Thomas, James D, et al., 1987. "Disease, lifestyle and consanguinity in 58 American Gypsies", *The Lancet*, August 25, pp 377–9.

Tipler, Derek, 1968. "From nomads to nation", *Midstream*, August-September, pp 61–70

Turner, Ralph, 1927. "On the position of Romani in Indo-Aryan", *Journal of the Gypsy Lore Society*, third series, 5(4):145–183.

USGPO, 1946. *Nazi Conspiracy and Aggression*, Volume 3. Washington: US Government Printing Office.

Vaillant, J A, 1857. *Les Rômes: Historie Vraie des Vrais Bohémiens*. Paris: Dentu and Cie.

Vekerdi József, 1976. "The Gypsy's role in the preservation of non-Gypsy folklore", *Journal of the Gypsy Lore Society*, Fourth series, 1(2):79–86.

Vekerdi József, 1984. "The Vend Gypsy dialect in Hungary", *Acta Linguistica*, 34(1/2): 65–86.

Vekerdi József, 1988. "The Gypsies and the Gypsy problem in Hungary", *Hungarian Studies Review*, 15(2):13–26.

Walker, Barbara G, 1983. *The Woman's Encyclopedia of Myths and Secrets*. New York: Harper Row.

Wajs, Bronisława, 1950. *Krwawe Łzy: Co za Niemców Przeszliśmy na Wołyniu w 43 i 44 Roku*. Tarnów.

Washington, Booker T, 1901. *Up From Slavery*. New York: Doubleday, Page and Co.

Weckman, Saga, 1983. *Researching Gypsies: Advice from a Romni.* Document distributed at the Eleventh International Congress of Anthropological and Ethnological Sciences, Quebec, 22–25 August.

Wood, Manfri Fred, 1973. *In the Life of a Romany Gypsy.* London and Boston: Routledge and Kegan Paul.

Zygmant, Bill, 1974. "Indian Kathy, the girl who has gypsies in her soul: Riding out on a crusade to win back the Romanies' pride", *The Evening News*, London, Friday, September 27, p. 16.

Index

The *Interface Collection*

The *Interface Collection* was developed by the Centre for Gypsy Research at the Université René Descartes in Paris in association with publishers throughout Europe and with the support of the European Commission and the Council for Europe. The Centre for Gypsy Research is at the hub of a unique international publishing programme with volumes appearing in up to twelve European languages.

This has been severely curtailed since 2001 by the loss of EU funding for the work of the specialist editorial committees and for the translations organised by the Centre for Gypsy Research and as a result only those volumes which the publishers consider to be commercially viable can now be published. This at present excludes the concluding two volumes in the important series on the Gypsies during the Second World War and further volumes in the series on the Romani language.

For further details about the work of the Centre for Gypsy Research:

Centre de recherches tsiganes
Université René Descartes
45 rue des Saints-Pères
F – 75270 - PARIS Cedex 06,
France

Tel: +33 331 42862112
Fax: +33 1 42862065
E-mail: crt@paris5.sorbonne.fr

Web address: http://www.eurrenet.com/

A list of the volumes published so far with the addresses of the publishers follows.

Titles in the *Interface Collection*

Each volume in the *Interface Collection* is published in up to twelve languages (see list of publishers). The English language editions of the *Interface Collection* are published by the University of Hertfordshire Press. Where an English language edition has not been published details of other language editions are given. The code in front of the ISBN identifies the publisher.

An updated version of this list can be seen on the web pages of the University of Hertfordshire Press at: http://www.herts.ac.uk/UHPress/interface.html

1	Marcel Kurtiàde	Śirpustik amare ćhibǎqiri (Pupil's book) with Teacher's manual CRDP: ISBN 2-86565-074-X
2	Antonio Gómez Alfaro	The Great Gypsy Round-up PG: ISBN 84-87347-12-6
3	Donald Kenrick	Gypsies: from the Ganges to the Thames UHP: ISBN 1-902806-23-9
4	E. M. Lopes da Costa	On Gypsies: a bibliography of works in Portuguese PG: ISBN 84-87347-11-8
5	Marielle Danbakli	Roma, Gypsies: Texts issued by International Institutions UHP: ISBN 1-902806-15-8
6	Bernard Leblon	Gypsies and Flamenco UHP: ISBN 1-902806-05-0
7	David Mayall	English Gypsies and State Policies UHP: ISBN 0-900458-64-X
8	D. Kenrick, G. Puxon	Gypsies under the Swastika UHP: ISBN 0-900458-65-8
9	Giorgio Viaggio	Storia degli Zingari in Italia ANICIA/CSZ: ISBN 88-900078-9-3
10	D. Kenrick, G. Puxon	Bibaxtale Berśa PG: ISBN 84-87347-15-0
11	Jean-Pierre Liégeois	School Provision for Ethnic Minorities: The Gypsy Paradigm UHP: ISBN 0-900458-88-7
12	Joint authorship	From "Race Science" to the Camps The Gypsies during the Second World War – 1 UHP: ISBN 0-900458-78-X
13	Joint authorship	In the Shadow of the Swastika The Gypsies during the Second World War – 2 UHP: ISBN 0-900458-85-2
14	G. Donzello, B. M. Karpati	Un ragazzo zingaro nella mia classe ANICIA: 88-900078-4-2
15	A. Gómez Alfaro E. M. Lopes da Costa	Deportaciones de Gitanos PG: ISBN 84-87347-18-5
	Sharon Floate	Ciganos e degredos SE: ISBN 972-8339-24-0
16	Ilona Lacková	A false dawn – My life as a Gypsy woman in Slovakia UHP: ISBN 1-902806-00-X
17	Jean-Pierre Liégeois	Ромц, Цъгани, Чергари LIT: ISBN 954-8537-63-X Roma, Sinti, Fahrende PA: ISBN 3-88402-289-X Romák, cigányok, utazók PONT: ISBN 963-9312-43-6

18	Reimar Gilsenbach	Von Tschudemann zu Seemann
		Zwei Prozesse aus der Geschichte deutscher Sinti
		PA: ISBN 3-88402-202-4
19	Jeremy Sandford	Rokkering to the Gorjios
		UHP: ISBN 1-902806-04-2
20	Joint authorship	Europe mocks Racism, International Anthology of
		Anti-Racist Humour (multiple editions) PG
21	Joint authorship	What is the Romani language?
		UHP: ISBN 1-902806-06-9
22	Elena Marushiakova	Gypsies in the Ottoman Empire
		UHP: ISBN 1-902806-02-6
23	Joint authorship	La Chiesa cattolica e gli Zingari
		ANICIA/CSZ ISBN 88-900078-5-0
24	Joint authorship	Que sorte, Ciganos na nossa escola!
		SE: ISBN 972-8339-29-1
25	Ian Hancock,	The Roads of the Roma: a PEN anthology of Gypsy
	Siobhan Dowd, Rajko Djuric	Writers UHP: ISBN 0-900458-90-9
	This English language edition was published outside the *Interface Collection*	
26	Santino Spinelli	Baxtaló Divès ANICIA: ISBN 88-7346-009-7
27	Emmanuel Filhol	La mémoire et l'oubli: l'internement des Tsiganes en
		France 1940–46 HAM: ISBN 2-7475-1399-8
28	Ian Hancock	We are the Romani People
		UHP: ISBN 1-902806-19-0
29	Alyosha Taikon,	From coppersmith to nurse:
	Gunilla Lundgren	Alyosha, the son of a Gypsy chief
		UHP: 1-902806-22-0
30	Ján Cangár	L'udia z rodiny
		Rómov manusa andar e familia Roma
		CROCUS: 80-88992-42-7
31	Josef Muscha Müller	Und weinen draf ich auch nicht...
		PA: 3-88402-284-9

Série Rukun / The Rukun Series

Eric Hill's popular *Spot the Dog* books in Romani

O Rukun ʒal and-i skòla	Research and Action Group on Romani Linguistics
	RB: ISBN 2-9507850-1-8
Kaj si o Rukun amaro?	Research and Action Group on Romani Linguistics
	RB: ISBN 2-9507850-2-6
Spot's Big Book of Words in Romani, French and English	
	Research and Action Group on Romani Linguistics
	RB: ISBN 2-9507850-3-4
Spot's Big Book of Words in Romani and Spanish	
	Research and Action Group on Romani Linguistics
	PG: ISBN 84-87347-22-3

Publishers' addresses

ANICIA
Via San Francesco a Ripa, 62
I – 00153 – Roma , Italy
web site:
http://members.it.tripod.de/anicia

CRDP – Centre Régional de
Documentation Pédagogique
Midi-Pyrénées
3 rue Roquelaine
F – 31069 – Toulouse Cedex, France
web site: http://www.crdp-toulouse.fr

CROCUS – Vydavate°stvo CROCUS Nové
Zámky
Stefan Safranek
Bernolákovo nám. 27
SK - 940 51 - Nové Zámky
web site:
http://www.crocus.sk

EA – Editura Alternative
Casa Presei, Corp. A, Et. 6
Pia a Presei Libere, 1
RO – 71341 - Bucureşti 1, Bulgaria

EK – Editions Kastaniotis
11, Zalogou
GR – 106 78 – Athèns, Greece
web site: http://www.kastaniotis.com

HAM – Editions L'Harmattan
5-7 rue de l'Ecole Polytechnique
F – 75005 – Paris, France
web site:
http://www.editions-
harmattan.fr

IBIS – Ibis Grafika
Sasa Krnic
IV. Ravnice 25
10 000 Zagreb
Croatia
web site:
http://www.ibis-grafika.hr

LIT – Litavra
163 A – Rakovski
BG – 1000 – Sofia, Romania

PA – Edition Parabolis
Schliemannstraße 23
D – 10437 Berlin, Germany
web site: http://www.emz-berlin.de

PG – Editorial Presencia Gitana
Valderrodrigo, 76 y 78
E – 28039 – Madrid, Spain
web site:
http://www.presenciagitana.org

PONT – Pont Kiadó
Pf 215
H – 1300 Budapest 3, Hungary
web site: http://www.pontkiado.com

SE – Entreculturas / Secretariado
Coordenador dos Programas de Educação
Multicultural
Trav. das Terras de Sant'Ana, 15 – 1°
PT – 1250 – Lisboa, Portugal
web site:
http//www.min-edu.pt/entreculturas

UHP – University of Hertfordshire Press
Learning and Information Services,
College Lane – Hatfield
UK – Hertfordshire AL10 9AB, Britain
web site:
http://www.herts.ac.uk/UHPress

VUP – Univerzita Palackého v
Olomouci – Vydavatelství /
Palacky University Press
Krížkovského 8
CZ – 771 47 – Olomouc, Czech Republic

Distributor for some Rukun titles:
RB – Rromani Baxt
22, rue du Port
F – 63000 Clermont-Ferrand, France

The University of Hertfordshire Press is the only university press committed to developing a major publishing programme on social, cultural and political aspects of the Romani and other Gypsy people who migrated from north west India at the beginning of the last millennium and are now found on every continent. Recent titles include:

Between Past and Future: the Roma of Central and Eastern Europe
Edited by Will Guy
ISBN 1-902806-07-7 £18.99
This important new study challenges popular misconceptions, analysing how and why Roma have become victims of political and economic restructuring following the overthrow of Communist rule.

A false dawn: my life as a Gypsy woman in Slovakia
Ilona Lackova (Interface Collection, Volume 16)
ISBN 1-902806-00-X £11.99
The inspirational life story of a remarkable woman transcribed and edited from recordings in Romani. The author witnessed the destruction of the Romani culture, language and way of life in the 'false dawn' of the post-war Communist era.

What is the Romani Language?
Peter Bakker et al (Interface Collection, Volume 21)
ISBN 1-902806-06-9 £11.99
This introductory guide by an international group of specialists in the Romani language describes its origin, current use, the way it is taught and the beginnings of Romani literature and films.

The Roads of the Roma: a PEN Anthology of Gypsy writers
Edited by Ian Hancock, Siobhan Dowd and Rajko Djuric
ISBN 0-900458-90-9 £11.99
Forty-three poems and prose extracts, most appearing in English for the first time, are arranged alongside an 800-year chronology of repression. What emerges is a portrait of a people struggling to preserve their identity in a hostile world.

Gypsies and Flamenco: the emergeance of the art of flamenco in Andalusia
Bernard Leblon (Interface Collection, Volume 6)
ISBN 0-902806-05-0 £9.99
Gypsies and Flamenco celebrates the passion of flamenco and pays its respects to hundreds of flamenco artists, any of whom can trace their roots back to a network of families so closely interwoven that in the end they constitute a single entity. A new section gives substantial biographical notes on 200 great gitano flamenco artists. This, together with an expanded glossary of flamenco terms and lists of flamenco CDs and video, makes *Gypsies and Flamenco* an indispensable resource for flamenco enthusiasts.

Shared Sorrows: a Gypsy family remembers the Holocaust
Toby Sonneman
ISBN 1-902806-10-7 £12.00
This powerful beautifully written book interweaves the story of the author's own Jewish family with that of the members of an extended family of Sinti survivors of the Holocaust which she came to know in Munich.

Gypsies under the Swastika
Donald Kenrick and Grattan Puxon (Interface Collection, Volume 8)
ISBN 0-900458-65-8 £9.99
The most comprehensive and up-to-date single-volume account of the fate of the Gypsies in the Holocaust.

Gypsies in the Ottoman Empire: a contribution to the history of the Balkans
Elena Marushiakova and Vesselin Popov (Interface Collection, Volume 22)
ISBN 1-902806-02-6 £11.99
The European part of the Ottoman Empire – the Balkans – has often been called the second motherland of the Gypsies. From this region Gypsies moved westwards taking with them inherited Balkan cultural models and traditions.

Scholarship and the Gypsy struggle: commitment in Romani Studies
Edited by Thomas Acton
ISBN 1-902806-01-8 £17.99
This book marks the development of a new, authoritative academic approach to Romani Studies which locates itself in the problems identified by the Romani people themselves.

Moving On: the Gypsies and Travellers of Britain
Donald Kenrick and Colin Clark
ISBN 0-900458-99-2 £9.99
The only general introduction to the struggle of Gypsies to survive as a people in Britain today.

Smoke in the Lanes
Dominic Reeve
ISBN 1-902806-24-7 £9.99
A classic account of the reality of life as a Gypsy in the fifties when Travellers lived in horse-drawn wagons and stopped by the wayside in quiet country lanes, but were often driven to 'atch' besides main highways as so many of the old stopping-places were fenced off or built upon. This book is full of stories of life on the road and descriptions of colourful characters living for the present despite constant harassment by police and suspicious landowners.

Gaining Ground: law reform for Gypsies and Travellers
Edited by Rachel Morris and Luke Clements (Traveller Law Research Unit, Cardiff Law School)
ISBN 0-900458-98-4 £17.00
An agenda for reform based on the proposals of professionals and of Gypsies and Travellers themselves.

Roma, Gypsies: Texts issued by International Institutions
Compiled by Marielle Danbakli (Interface Collection Volume 5)
ISBN 1-902806-15-8 £14.99
A new edition of this essential reference work for libraries, government departments and NGOs of the texts issued on Roma (Gypsies) by all the major international institutions from the European Union to the United Nations.

For further details see:

http://www.herts.ac.uk/UHPress/Gypsies.html

Or request a copy of our catalogue from:

University of Hertfordshire Press
Learning and Information Services
University of Hertfordshire
College Lane
Hatfield   Tel: +44 1707-284654
AL10 9AB   Fax: +44 1707-284666
United Kingdom   E-mail: UHPress@herts.ac.uk